CSS3

Pocket Primer

LICENSE, DISCLAIMER OF LIABILITY, AND LIMITED WARRANTY

CSS3

Pocket Primer

Oswald Campesato

MERCURY LEARNING AND INFORMATION

Dulles, Virginia
Boston, Massachusetts
New Delhi

Publisher: David Pallai
Mercury Learning and Information
22841 Quicksilver Drive
Dulles, VA 20166
info@merclearning.com
www.merclearning.com
800-232-0223

O. Campesato. *CSS3 Pocket Primer.*
ISBN: 978-1-938549-68-7

The publisher recognizes and respects all marks used by companies, manufacturers, and developers as a means to distinguish their products. All brand names and product names mentioned in this book are trademarks or service marks of their respective companies. Any omission or misuse (of any kind) of service marks or trademarks, etc. is not an attempt to infringe on the property of others.

Library of Congress Control Number: 2016951110

161718321   Printed in the United States of America

Our titles are available for adoption, license, or bulk purchase by institutions, corporations, etc.

For additional information, please contact the Customer Service Dept. at 800-232-0223(toll free).

All of our titles are available in digital format at *authorcloudware.com* and other digital vendors. The sole obligation of Mercury Learning and Information to the purchaser is to replace the book, based on defective materials or faulty workmanship, but not based on the operation or functionality of the product.

I'd like to dedicate this book to my parents –
may this bring joy and happiness into their lives.

CONTENTS

On the Companion Disc
Appendix A: jQuery Concepts
Appendix B: CSS Frameworks and Toolkits

PREFACE

WHAT IS THE PRIMARY VALUE PROPOSITION FOR THIS BOOK?

This book is primarily about CSS3, along with some of the technologies that can be "combined" with CSS3. In fact, there are several non-CSS3 chapters in this book, including one SVG chapter and one chapter that delves into HTML5 Canvas and CSS3. In addition, several chapters contain optional sections that show you how to combine jQuery with CSS3 and also jQuery with SVG. If you are unfamiliar with jQuery, you can read the Appendix that provides an introduction to jQuery. Another Appendix contains an introduction to an assortment of topics, such as frameworks for CSS3, SASS and LESS, Bootstrap 4, Material Design, and CSSLint.

WHAT IS THE FORMAT FOR THIS BOOK?

The answer to this question is important, because you obviously want to determine how much of the material in this book will be useful and relevant to you. First, this book is not a reference guide of CSS3 syntax, nor does this book contain any "cheat sheets" (but you can probably find the latter online). Although the format bears a very slight resemblance to a "cookbook" style, this book does not provide an extensive set of how-to code samples that solve many common tasks that you can probably find on Stackoverflow. Instead, the code samples in this book illustrate some "core" features of CSS3, and are supplemented with interesting effects that are possible in CSS3. Indeed, some code samples create effects that you are unlikely to find anywhere else. Even though you probably will not use all of the examples in this book, you will learn about various coding techniques, and perhaps you will be able to take advantage of them in order to craft your own variations for your Web pages.

WHAT DO I NEED TO KNOW FOR THIS BOOK?

The most important prerequisite is familiarity with HTML and basic CSS. In some cases (such as the examples in Chapter 6), familiarity with basic JavaScript is definitely necessary in order to understand the code samples. One way to get a better idea about this book is to glance through some of the code samples to get an idea of how much is familiar to you and how much is new for you. If you feel overwhelmed by too many unfamiliar concepts, then it's probably advisable to select a different book. On the other hand, if you feel that the material is new yet within your grasp, you can fill potential gaps (obviously details vary in this book) by reading online tutorials. The decision making process regarding the purchase of this book is obviously important to you, and satisfied customers are important to the publisher and the author.

THE TARGET AUDIENCE

This book is intended to reach an international audience of readers with highly diverse backgrounds in various age groups. While many readers know how to read English, their native spoken language is not English (which could be their second, third, or even fourth language). Consequently, this book uses standard English rather than colloquial expressions that might be confusing to those readers. As you know, many people learn by different types of imitation, which includes reading, writing, or hearing new material (yes, some basic videos are also available). This book takes these points into consideration in order to provide a comfortable and meaningful learning experience for the intended readers.

GETTING THE MOST FROM THIS BOOK

Some people learn well from prose, others learn well from sample code (and lots of it), which means that there's no single style that can be used for everyone.

Moreover, some people want to start by launching the HTML Web pages, see what they render, and then return to the code to delve into the details (and conversely, other people use the opposite approach).

In order to provide meaningful content for both types of people, this book contains a mixture of code samples: some are short, some are long, and other code samples "build" from earlier code samples.

The goal is to show (and not just tell) you a variety of visual effects that are possible, some of which you might not find anywhere else. You benefit from this approach because you can pick and choose the visual effects and the code that creates those visual effects.

HOW WAS THE CODE FOR THIS BOOK TESTED?

The code samples in this book have been tested in a Google Chrome browser (version v51) on a Macbook Pro with OS X 10.14. Unless otherwise noted, no special browser-specific features were used, which means that the code samples ought to work in Chrome on other platforms, and also in other modern browsers. Exceptions are due to limitations in the cross-platform availability of specific features of SVG itself. Although the code also works in several earlier versions of Chrome on a Macbook Pro, you need to test the code on your platform and browser (especially if you are using Internet Explorer).

Another point to keep in mind is that all references to "Web Inspector" refer to the Web Inspector in Chrome, which differs from the Web Inspector in Safari. If you are using a different (but still modern) browser or an early version of Chrome, you might need to check online for the sequence of keystrokes that you need to follow to launch and view the Web Inspector. Navigate to this link for additional useful information:

http://benalman.com/projects/javascript-debug-console-log/

WHY DOES THIS BOOK HAVE 200 PAGES INSTEAD OF 500 PAGES?

This book is part of the *Pocket Primer Series* whose books are generally between 200 and 250 pages. Second, the target audience consists of readers ranging from beginners to intermediate in terms of their knowledge of HTML and JavaScript. At the same time, one of the primary rules of exposition of virtually any kind is "show, don't tell." While this rule is not taken literally in this book, it's the motivation for showing first and telling second. If the adage "a picture is worth a thousand words" is true, then this book endeavors to provide both the pictures and the words.

COMPANION DISC

The companion disc included with the book contains all the code samples to save you time and effort from the error-prone process of manually typing code into an HTML Web page. In addition, there are situations in which you might not have easy access to companion disc. Furthermore, the code samples in the book provide explanations that are not available on the companion disc. *All of the files on the companion disc are available for downloading by writing to the publisher at info@merclearning.com.*

DOES THIS BOOK CONTAIN PRODUCTION-LEVEL CODE SAMPLES?

The primary purpose of the code samples in this book is to illustrate various features of CSS3. Clarity has higher priority than writing more compact code that is more difficult to understand (and possibly more prone to bugs). If you decide to use any of the code in this book in a production website, you ought to subject that code to the same rigorous analysis as the other parts of your HTML Web pages.

WHY ARE THE SCREENSHOTS IN BLACK AND WHITE?

The black and white images are less costly than the original color images, and therefore their inclusion means that this book is available at a lower cost. *However, the color images are available on the companion disc,* along with supplemental code samples that render in color when you launch them in a browser.

OTHER RELATED BOOKS BY THE AUTHOR

1) HTML5 Canvas and CSS3:

http://www.amazon.com/HTML5-Canvas-CSS3-Graphics-Primer/ dp/1936420341

2) jQuery, HTML5, and CSS3:

http://www.amazon.com/jQuery-HTML5-Mobile-Desktop-Devices/ dp/1938549031

3) HTML5 Pocket Primer:

http://www.amazon.com/HTML5-Pocket-Primer-Oswald-Campesato/ dp/1938549104

4) jQuery Pocket Primer:

http://www.amazon.com/dp/1938549147

The following open source projects contain code samples that supplement the material in various chapters of this book:

https://github.com/ocampesato/css3-graphics
https://github.com/ocampesato/d3-graphics
https://github.com/ocampesato/html5-graphics
https://github.com/ocampesato/jquery-css3-graphics
https://github.com/ocampesato/jquery-graphics
https://github.com/ocampesato/react-svg-gsapi
https://github.com/ocampesato/react-svg-graphics-14
https://github.com/ocampesato/svg-filters-graphicshttps://github.com/ ocampesato/svg-graphics
https://github.com/ocampesato/threejs-graphics

CHAPTER 1

HTML5 FEATURES

This chapter introduces you to some features of HTML5 and HTML5-specific elements for semantic markup. You will also learn about some websites that provide useful information, such as browser support for HTML5 features, and also get some information about the W3C and the WHATWG standards groups.

One question must be addressed before you read this chapter: why does this CSS3 book contain an introductory chapter about HTML5? First, CSS exists entirely inside the context of a website: unlike JavaScript, there is no "server side" CSS. Second, there are many technologies that are considered part of the HTML5 "umbrella," and they vary considerably in terms of the complexity of their associated APIs. Third, it's certainly possible that you will encounter JavaScript (if you haven't already) and also need to learn some rudimentary aspects of JavaScript. In fact, when such content is deemed relevant and useful, some of the chapters in this book contain JavaScript-related sections (often marked "optional").

The first part of this chapter introduces HTML5, browser support, and two HTML5 Working Groups. The second part describes the technologies that are part of HTML5, differences between HTML4 and HTML5, some useful online tools, and feature detection. The third part of this chapter shows you a simple HTML5 website, new HTML5 elements, and Semantic Markup. The final part of this chapter introduces you to WAI ARIA, experimental features, and mobile support.

Another point to keep in mind is that there are multiple modern browsers available, all of which provide very good support for HTML and CSS. However, due to space and time limitations and the number of topics to cover, Chrome was chosen as the primary browser to test the code samples in this book. Although the code samples in this particular book will most likely work in other modern browsers, you can check whether or not a CSS feature is supported in a given browser here: *www.caniuse.com*.

Lastly, if you decide to skip the initial high-level sections of this chapter, the section called "A Simple HTML Website" contains an example of an HTML website, followed by a description of its contents. Later you can obviously return to the sections that you skipped in this chapter.

WHAT IS HTML5?

Despite the simplicity of the question, the answer is imprecise: HTML5 consists of a mixture of technologies, some of which are formally included in the HTML5 specification, and some which are not part of the specification. There are few people who seem to know the "definition" of HTML5, and perhaps that's why Peter Paul Koch (creator of the `quirksmode` website) wryly suggested that "whatever web technology you're working on that's cool right now . . . that's HTML5." As you will discover, HTML5 means different things to different people, so don't be surprised if you cannot get one consistent "definition" of HTML5 (if only the situation were so simple!).

However, it's also true that HTML5 is the latest version of HTML that is backward compatible with most features of earlier versions of HTML markup. In addition to its plugin-free architecture, HTML5 provides a wealth of new features: new tags for audio, video, and semantic markup; new input types and validation for forms; local and session storage; support for graphics-based APIs in `Canvas`; and communication-related techniques such as server sent events and web sockets. Most of the technologies listed in the previous sentence are outside the scope of this book, so there's no need to worry if they are unfamiliar to you.

Although CSS3 is not a part of HTML5, many people consider it to be an important (perhaps even integral) part of websites. Indeed, CSS3 is a core aspect of many visual design components of a website or application. As you will see in Chapters 2 through 4, CSS3 provides support for rich visual effects, including 2D/3D graphics and animation.

With regard to HTML markup, the good news is that the new HTML5 semantic tags provide more meaningful information about the purpose of each section in an HTML5 website, which can be discerned much more easily than websites written in HTML4. You will see an example of using some of these semantic tags later in this chapter.

In addition, HTML was initially designed with the goal of running HTML websites on desktop devices as well as mobile devices. Since 1996 CSS itself has contained media attributes (such as handheld) that reflect this early thinking about the purpose of HTML.

Web-based mobile applications do not support push notifications. There are some Android-specific features, such as adding ringtones, performing notifications, or changing the wallpaper that are typically user features.

There is one other point to keep in mind: the specification for HTML 4.01 (the predecessor to HTML5) was introduced in 1999, so HTML5 represents the largest advance in HTML in years, and perhaps the inclusion of other technologies was inevitable. There is a great deal of excitement surrounding HTML5. Indeed, the enthusiasm for HTML5 has accelerated the speed with which HTML became a formal specification based on open standards.

Browser Support for HTML5

The `WebKit`-based browsers (Chrome and Safari), as well as Mozilla Firefox, Opera, IE10, and Microsoft Edge support many HTML features, on desktops as well as mobile devices. As for mobile devices, a very good website that lists the HTML features (including the ones that have been discussed in this chapter) that are supported by mobile browsers is here:
http://mobilehtml5.org/.
Currently Safari on iOS supports twenty-eight features whereas the Android supports twenty-four features (other browsers are listed as well).
Another good website that provides test results of HTML-related features on various mobile devices is here:
http://www.quirksmode.org/mobile/.
The preceding website is maintained by Peter Paul Koch (who is often called PPK), and he maintains websites with many test results, along with blog posts expressing his views about trends in HTML5 and the mobile space.

WHICH TECHNOLOGIES ARE INCLUDED IN HTML5?

The following list contains a combination of technologies that are formally included in the HTML5 specification, as well as several other technologies that are frequently associated with HTML5:

- Canvas 2D
- CSS3
- Drag-and-Drop (DnD)
- File API
- Geolocation
- Microdata
- Offline Applications
- Server Sent Events (SSE)
- SVG
- Web Intents
- Web Messaging
- Web Storage
- Web Sockets
- Web Workers

There are other technologies that are often associated with HTML5, including WebGL and XHR2 (XmlHTTPRequest Level 2).

Keep in mind that the status of some of these technologies will change, so be sure to visit the link with the details of the W3C specification for each of these technologies in order to find their most recent status.

DIFFERENCES BETWEEN HTML4 TAGS AND HTML5 TAGS

Broadly speaking, HTML5 differs from earlier versions of HTML in the following ways:

- Does not support some HTML4.x elements
- Provides support for new elements
- Simplifies some existing elements
- Includes support for custom attributes

The following are some new elements in HTML5: `<article>`, `<aside>`, `<audio>`, `<canvas>`, `<command>`, `<datalist>`, `<details>`, `<dialog>`, `<figure>`, `<footer>`, `<header>`, `<keygen>`, `<mark>`, `<meter>`, `<nav>`, `<output>`, `<progress>`, `<rp>`, `<rt>`, `<ruby>`, `<section>`, `<source>`, `<time>`, and `<video>`.

The HTML elements that are not recommended for new work in HTML5 (many of which have been replaced with CSS styling) include the following: `<acronym>`, `<applet>`, `<basefont>`, `<big>`, `<center>`, `<dir>`, `<font>`, `<frame>`, `<frameset>`, `<noframes>`, `<s>`, `<strike>`, `<tt>`, and `<u>`.

You are probably already aware of the new HTML5 `<audio>` element and HTML5 `<video>` element, and later in this chapter you'll see examples of how to use these elements in HTML5 websites.

One important new HTML5 feature is custom data attributes, which always have a `data-` prefix. This support for custom data attributes provides HTML5 markup with some of the functionality that is available in XML, which enables code to process custom tags and their values and also pass validation at the same time.

If you want additional details, a full list of the differences between HTML5 and HTML4 is in the following W3C document:
http://dev.w3.org/html5/html4-differences/.

USEFUL ONLINE TOOLS FOR HTML5 DEVELOPMENT

Before delving into the new HTML5 elements that are discussed in this chapter, you need to know about the online tools that can assist in creating well-written HTML. These tools are available because of one important fact: modern browsers differ in terms of their support for HTML5 features (for desktop browsers and also for mobile browsers). Fortunately, tools such as

`Modernizr` enable you to detect HTML5 feature support in modern browsers using simple JavaScript code.

Modernizr

`Modernizr` is a very useful tool for HTML5-related feature detection in various browsers, and its home page is here:

http://www.modernizr.com/.

In case you didn't already know, server-side "browser sniffing" used to be a popular technique for detecting the browser that you were using to render a particular website, but this technique is not as accurate (or as "clean") due to rapidly changing implementations in browsers. Indeed, the most popular websites that check for HTML5 support use feature detection and not browser sniffing.

At some point you will start using JavaScript in your HTML5 websites (indeed, you probably do so already), and `Modernizr` provides a programmatic way to check for many HTML5 and CSS3 features in different browsers.

In order to use `Modernizr`, include the following code snippet in the <head> element of your websites:

```
<script src="modernizr.min.js" type="text/javascript">
</script>
```

The following type of code block illustrates one way that you can use `Modernizr` in an HTML page:

```
if(Modernizr.canvas) {
  // canvas is available
  // do something here
} else {
  // canvas is not available
  // do something else here
}
```

NOTE *Unlike many scripts that can be inserted after the body of the page,* Modernizr *is designed to run before the page is rendered and before any other scripts.*

Navigate to the `Modernizr` home page where you can read the documentation, tutorials, and details regarding the set of feature detection.

Caniuse

The following website ("When Can I Use . . .") is extremely useful because it provides information regarding support for many HTML5 features in modern browsers:

http://www.caniuse.com.

Currently there are two main tabs on this website. The first (and default) tab is divided into a number of sections (CSS, HTML5, SVG, JS API, and

Other), and each section contains a list of technical items that are hyperlinks to other websites that provide detailed information.

The second tab on this website is called "tables," and when you click on this tab you will see a tabular display of information in a set of tables. The columns in each table are modern browsers, the rows specify features, and the cells in the tables provide the browser version numbers where the specified features are supported.

The following website also provides very useful information regarding HTML5:

http://html5boilerplate.com/.

USING FEATURE DETECTION IN HTML WEBSITES

Browser or UA sniffing refers to parsing the User Agent string available in every browser, and then using the results to determine how to proceed. However, browser sniffing is unreliable, and it's been replaced by feature detection, which checks for the availability of features in a browser. Feature detection can treat new browsers in the same manner as current browsers, whereas browser sniffing uses hard-coded strings (which might also contain regular expressions), so new code must be added whenever a new browser becomes available.

The four basic ways to detect for HTML5 functions are listed here:

- Check for the property on a global object
- Check for the property on an element you create
- Check that a method returns a correct value
- Check that an element retains a value

Every HTML5 document is displayed in a global element, which is usually called the `navigator` or the `window`. You can use a global element to test whether or not offline web applications are supported in a browser as shown here:

```
if(window.applicationCache) {
   console.logwrite("Your browser supports offline apps.");
} else {
   console.log("Your browser does not support offline web
      apps.");
}
```

If your browser supports the `applicationCache` item, then it can use features such as online/offline detection, the offline application cache, and so forth.

An example of testing whether or not an element retains a value is shown here:

```
var div = document.createElement('div');
div.style.cssText = "background-
color:rgba(150,255,150,.5)";
if(!!~(''' + div.style.backgroundColor).indexOf('rgba')){
```

```
// rgba is supported so do something here
}
```

A SIMPLE HTML WEBSITE

In addition to introducing many new semantic elements, HTML5 has simplified several elements, including the <DOCTYPE> declaration and the attributes lang and charset. Listing 1.1 displays Sample1.html, which is an HTML5 website that illustrates the simplified syntax of HTML5.

LISTING 1.1 Sample1.html

```
<!doctype html>
<html lang="en">
 <head>
  <meta charset="utf-8">
  <title>This is HTML5</title>
 </head>

 <body>
   <div id="outer"></div>
 <body>
</html>
```

Listing 1.1 contains an HTML5 <!DOCTYPE> element whose simple structure is very intuitive and easy to remember, especially in comparison to the syntax for an HTML4 <!DOCTYPE> element (try to construct one from memory!). This markup is backward compatible: it triggers standards mode in all browsers that have standards mode (versus quirks mode) and it also tells the browser to use the special HTML5 parsing mode.

In addition, the <meta> tag and its attributes lang and charset are simpler than their counterparts in earlier versions of HTML. Note that HTML5 supports the new syntax as well as the earlier syntax, so your existing HTML pages will be recognized in HTML5.

NEW HTML5 ELEMENTS

This section discusses some of the useful new elements in HTML5, which include semantic-related elements, the <video> element, and the <audio> element. The new types for the <input> element are discussed in the section for HTML5 forms (later in this chapter). A modest knowledge of the new HTML5 tags is required in order to follow the examples in this book, so you can skim through this section if you do not require extensive knowledge of HTML5 elements.

Semantic Markup HTML5 Elements

HTML5 provides new elements for "semantic markup" that are designed to provide more meaningful structure in your HTML5 websites. Some of these new tags are: `<section>`, `<article>`, `<aside>`, `<nav>`, `<header>`, `<canvas>`, `<video>`, `<audio>`, `<time>`, `<figure>`, and `<figcaption>`.

For example, the HTML5 `<section>` tag can be used as a "container" for a document, whereas the HTML5 `<article>` tag is well-suited for representing the content of a newspaper article or a blog post. The HTML5 `<header>` tag and HTML5 `<footer>` tag represent the header and footer of an HTML5 `<section>` tag. The HTML5 `<aside>` tag contains information that is somewhat related to the primary content of a website (similar in nature to a "by the way" type of comment).

The HTML5 `<nav>` tag supports navigation for a section of a document in a website. Other new tags include the HTML5 `<dialog>` tag for marking up conversations and the HTML5 `<figure>` tag for associating a caption for videos or graphics (which is useful for search engines).

The semantics of these tags are straightforward, yet there are some subtler aspects that you will learn as you gain experience with HTML5 websites.

Semantic markup also includes WAI-ARIA (Web Accessibility Initiative – Accessible Rich Internet Applications). In brief, WAI-ARIA is a "bridging" technology that clarifies semantics of assistive technologies. The WAI-ARIA specification describes the roles, states, and properties that define accessible user interface elements, which are described (along with `aria-*` attributes on HTML elements) here:

http://dev.w3.org/html5/spec/wai-aria.html.

Article versus Section: How Are They Used?

The semantics of the HTML5 `<article>` element and the HTML5 `<section>` element are complex, partly because they can be nested in each other: an `<article>` element can contain one or more `<section>` elements, and each of those `<section>` elements can contain one or more `<article>` elements. While it's possible to devise a "hack" to disambiguate the logical relationship of these elements in a given HTML5 website, no standard convention exists right now. Another factor is the manner in which these two HTML elements are treated by the Document Outlining Algorithm for creating outlines in HTML websites, which is described here:

http://coding.smashingmagazine.com/2011/08/16/html5-and-the-document-outlining-algorithm.

For simple HTML5 websites, the `<article>` element and the `<section>` element will behave in a reasonable manner, but for more complex HTML5 websites, the results might be unexpected (or unwanted). Before you use the `<section>` and `<article>` elements for content in an HTML5 website, think of the logical relationship of the content in order to determine the structural layout of your HTML5 website. If there is any possibility for confusion, it might also be helpful to include a comment section to make it easier for other people to understand the rationale for the layout of your HTML5 website. In any case, it's worth spending some time learning about these elements and also about the Document Outlining Algorithm.

Why Use Semantic Markup?

There are at least two reasons for using semantic tags in your websites. First, semantic tags can help you understand the structure of a website and the purpose of a section of markup. Second, the use of semantic tags makes it easier for you to programmatically locate and manage sets of logically similar sections of code (such as <nav> elements, <aside> elements, and so forth). Third, screen-readers and search engines can use these tags to separate the content from navigation in a website. These are several of the more important reasons for using semantic markup, and you can probably think of other reasons as well.

A Simple Website with Semantic Markup

Listing 1.2 displays the contents of SemanticMarkup1.html, which illustrates how to use HTML5 semantic markup.

LISTING 1.2 SemanticMarkup1.html

```
<!DOCTYPE HTML>
<html>
<head>
   <meta charset="utf-8">
   <title>Examples of HTML5 Semantic Markup </title>
 </head>

 <body>
  <article> <!-- start article #1 -->
    <header>
       <h1>An HTML5 CSS3 Canvas Graphics Primer</h1>
    </header>

    <header>
        <aside style="font-size:larger;font-style:italic;
           color:red;float:right;width:150px;">
          The book is available on Amazon as well as
             MercLearning.
        </aside>
<p>This book covers the features of HTML5 Canvas graphics
and CSS3 graphics, and shows how to extend the power of
CSS3 with SVG.<p>
<p>The material is accessible to people with basic
knowledge of HTML and JavaScript, and more advanced users
will benefit from the examples of sophisticated CSS3 2D/3D
animation effects.</p>
<p>Learn how to create HTML5 Web sites that use Canvas,
CSS3, and SVG to render 2D shapes and Bezier curves, create
linear and radial gradients, apply transforms to 2D shapes
and JPG files, create animation effects, and generate 2D/3D
bar charts and line graphs.<p>
```

```
      <nav>
        <ul>
          <li><a href="http://www.amazon.ca/HTML5-Canvas-
              CSS3-Graphics-Primer/dp/1936420341">Amazon
              Link</a></li>
          <li><a href="http://www.merclearning.com/titles/
              html5_canvas_css3_graphics.html">
              MercLearning Link</a></li>
        </ul>
      </nav>

      <details>
        <summary>More Details About the Book</summary>
<p>The code samples in this book run on WebKit-based
browsers on desktops and tablets. A companion DVD contains
all the source code and color graphics in the book.</p>
      </details>
    </header>

    <section>
      <h3>Other Books by the Author</h3>
      <article> <!-- start article #2 -->
        <p>Previous books include: Java Graphics
Programming, Web 2.0 Fundamentals, SVG Fundamentals, and
Pro Android Flash.<p>
        <footer>
          <p>Posted by: Oswald Campesato</p>
        </footer>
        <details>
        <summary>More Details</summary>
        <p>Contact me for more detailed information</p>
        </details>
      </article> <!-- end article #2 -->

      <article> <!-- start article #3 -->
<p>SVCC (Silicon Valley Code Camp) is the biggest free
code camp in the world, and also a great way to meet like-
minded people who are interested in the latest trends in
technology.</p>
        <img src="ThreeSpheres1.png" width="200"
             height="100" />
      </article> <!-- end article #3 -->
    </section>
  </article> <!-- end article #1 -->
 </body>
</html>
```

The <body> tag in Listing 1.2 contains an HTML5 <article> tag that in turn contains two HTML5 <header> tags, where the second HTML5 <header> tag contains an HTML5 <aside>. The next part of Listing 1.2 contains an HTML5 <nav> element with three HTML <a> links for navigation.

Figure 1.1 displays the result of rendering the website SemanticMarkup1.html in a Chrome browser.

An HTML5 CSS3 Canvas Graphics Primer

This book covers the features of HTML5 Canvas graphics and CSS3 graphics, and shows how to extend the power of CSS3 with SVG.

The material is accessible to people with basic knowledge of HTML and JavaScript, and more advanced users will benefit from the examples of sophisticated CSS3 2D/3D animation effects.

Learn how to create HTML5 web pages that use Canvas, CSS3, and SVG to render 2D shapes and Bezier curves, create linear and radial gradients, apply transforms to 2D shapes and JPG files, create animation effects, and generate 2D/3D bar charts and line graphs.

The book is available on Amazon as well as MercLearning.

- Amazon Link
- MercLearning Link

► More Details About the Book

Other Books by the Author

Previous books include: Java Graphics Programming, Web 2.0 Fundamentals, SVG Fundamentals, and Pro Android Flash.

Posted by: Oswald Campesato

► More Details

SVCC (Silicon Valley Code Camp) is the biggest free code camp in the world, and also a great way to meet like-minded people who are interested in the latest trends in technology.

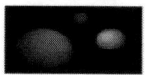

FIGURE 1.1 An HTML5 website with semantic markup in a Chrome browser.

Custom Data Attributes in HTML5

HTML5 supports custom data attributes, which effectively enable you to write HTML5 websites in which you can store custom data that is private to the website or application.

Listing 1.3 displays the contents of the website `CustomAtributes1.html`, which illustrate some of the custom attributes that are available in jQuery Mobile.

LISTING 1.3 CustomAttributes1.html

```
<!doctype html>
<html lang="en">
  <head>
   <meta charset="utf-8">
      <title>Hello World from jQueryMobile</title>
  </head>

  <body>
    <div id="page1" data-role="page">
      <header data-role="header" data-position="fixed">
        <h1>jQuery Mobile</h1>
      </header>

      <div class="content" data-role="content">
        <h3>Content Area</h3>
      </div>

      <footer data-role="footer" data-position="fixed">
        <h3>Fixed Footer</h3>
      </footer>
    </div>
  </body>
</html>
```

Listing 1.3 displays the structure of an HTML5 website for jQuery Mobile, but it is incomplete because it does not contain references to any jQuery JavaScript files or CSS stylesheets. The purpose of Listing 1.3 is to shows you the layout of a simple jQuery Mobile page, which in this case consists of one so-called "page view" along with some of the custom data attributes that are common in jQuery Mobile.

HTML5 VALIDATORS

HTML5 validators enable you to test HTML5 websites and mobile applications. Many types of validators for web applications are available, including:

- HTML validators: test the validity of your HTML
- Accessibility validators: test websites to determine how well they can be read by screen readers
- Code validators (aka lint): check your scripts, CSS, and API calls for accuracy
- Mobile validators: provide advice for improving pages for mobile devices. They often act as emulators as well.

In addition to the preceding list, there are other tools that can evaluate the "friendliness" of your website, such as:

- The W3C mobileOK Checker at *http://validator.w3.org/mobile*
- MobiReady at *http://ready.mobi/*

Both the W3C mobileOK Checker and mobiReady look at pages that are live on the Internet, and then give you a report of how they would perform on mobile devices.

WAI-ARIA

WAI-ARIA (Web Accessibility Initiative – Accessible Rich Internet Applications) is a W3C specification that specifies how to increase the accessibility of websites (including dynamic content) and user interface components developed with AJAX, HTML, JavaScript, and related technologies.

The WAI-ARIA specification defines support for accessible web applications, which involves markup extensions that are often attributes of HTML5 elements. Web developers can use these markup extensions to obtain more information about screen readers and other assistive technologies.

As a simple example, consider the following code snippet of an enhanced HTML `<li>` element from the ARIA specification that illustrates the use of the `role` and `aria-checked` attributes:

```
<li role="menuitemcheckbox" aria-checked="true">
  <img src="checked.gif" role="presentation" alt="">
  <!-- note: additional scripts required to toggle image
    source -->
```

```
Sort by Last Modified
</li>
```

The two new attributes in the preceding code snippet have no impact on the manner in which browsers render the <li> element. Browsers that support ARIA will add OS-specific accessibility information to the rendered <li> element and enable screen readers to read information aloud in a contextual manner.

You can get more information about the WAI-AIA specification here: *http://www.w3.org/TR/wai-aria/* and

http://www.techrepublic.com/blog/webmaster/a-checklist-for-web-accessibility-issues/2626.

HTML5 AND VARIOUS WORKING GROUPS

The W3C (World Wide Web Consortium), the WHATWG (Web Hypertext Application Technology Working Group), and the DAP (Device APIs Working Group) are organizations that provide the specifications and APIs for HTML5 and mobile devices that are covered in this book. In addition, the IETF (Internet Engineering Task Force) handles the networking standards (such as WebSockets, SPDY, CORS, and so forth), but not the actual APIs, and its home page is here:

https://www.ietf.org/.

The W3C is an international community for various membership, companies, and organizations to work together in order to develop Web standards. The W3C is directed by Web inventor Tim Berners-Lee and CEO Jeffrey Jaffe, and its home page is here:

http://www.w3.org.

Every proposal submitted to the W3C undergoes the following sequence in order to become a W3C Recommendation:

- Working Draft (WD)
- Candidate Recommendation (CR)
- Proposed Recommendation (PR)
- W3C Recommendation (REC)
- Later revisions

The HTML5-related technologies (listed earlier in this chapter) that have been submitted to the W3C are in different stages of the W3C "evaluation" process.

In essence, the WHATWG has the master specification, which the W3C HTML Working Group takes as the foundation for the "official" specification. The W3C synchronizes its work with the WHATWG, mostly reformatting to match its publication style (including breaking it into sub-specifications.)

The exact list of changes in the introduction to the WHATWG form of the specification is here:

http://www.whatwg.org/specs/web-apps/current-work/multipage/intro-duction.html#introduction.

The following link provides a list of HTML5 APIs and their most recent status updates:

http://www.w3.org/TR/.

SUMMARY

This chapter introduced you to HTML5, along with some technologies that are associated with HTML5. Next you learned about some of the differences between HTML5 and HTML4.01, some useful tools (such as Modernizr), and feature detection. Then you saw an example of a simple HTML5 Web page, which led to a discussion of new HTML elements and semantic markup in HTML. Finally, you learned some things about WAI-ARIA, the W3C, and the WHATWG.

CHAPTER 2

INTRODUCTION TO CSS3

This chapter introduces various aspects of CSS3, such as 2D transforms, graphics, and animation. Consequently, you need to have a reasonable grasp of CSS2 (i.e., how to define CSS selectors, the rules for selecting them with elements in HTML, etc.). If you are unfamiliar with CSS selectors, there are many introductory articles available through an Internet search. If you are convinced that CSS operates under confusing and seemingly arcane rules, then it's probably worth your while to read an online article about CSS box model rules, after which you will have a better understanding of the underlying logic of CSS.

The first part of the chapter starts with a brief overview of various CSS3 features, such as pseudo-selectors, pseudo-classes, and attribute selection. The second part of this chapter contains code samples that illustrate how to create shadow effects, how to render rectangles with rounded corners, and also how to use linear and radial gradients.

The third part of this chapter covers CSS3 transforms (scale, rotate, skew, and translate), along with code samples that illustrate how to apply transforms to HTML elements and to binary files. The final part of this chapter covers CSS3 support in browsers and briefly discusses the purpose of browser-specific prefixes for CSS3 features.

You can launch the code samples in this chapter in any browser on a desktop or a laptop; you can also view them on mobile devices, provided that you launch them in a browser that supports the CSS3 features that are used in the code samples.

CSS3 BROWSER SUPPORT

Before we delve into the details of CSS3, there are two important details that you need to know about defining CSS3-based selectors for use with

HTML. First, you need to know the CSS3 features that are available in different browsers. One of the best websites for determining browser support for CSS3 features is here:

http://caniuse.com/.

The preceding link contains tabular information regarding CSS3 support in many different browsers, which makes the information in that website very valuable.

Another highly useful tool that checks for CSS3 feature support is `Enhance.js`, which tests browsers to determine whether or not they can support a set of essential CSS and JavaScript properties, and then delivers features to those browsers that satisfy the test. You can download `Enhance.js` here:

https://github.com/filamentgroup/EnhanceJS.

QUICK OVERVIEW OF CSS3 FEATURES

CSS3 adopts a modularized approach involving multiple specifications for extending existing CSS2 functionality as well as supporting new functionality. The following link contains a list of all the completed specifications and drafts by the CSS WG (specifications and Working Groups are discussed in Chapter 1), along with their current status:

https://www.w3.org/Style/CSS/current-work.en.html.

In brief, CSS3 enables you to create boxes with rounded corners and shadow effects; create rich graphics effects using linear and radial gradients; detect portrait and landscape mode; detect the type of mobile device using media query selectors; and produce multicolumn text rendering and formatting.

In addition, CSS3 enables you to define sophisticated node selection rules in selectors using pseudo-classes, first or last child (`:first-child`, `:last-child`, `:first-of-type`, and `:last-of-type`), and also pattern-matching tests for attributes of elements. Several sections in this chapter contain examples of how to create such selection rules.

CSS3 PSEUDO CLASSES AND ATTRIBUTE SELECTION

This brief section contains examples of some pseudo-classes, followed by snippets that show you how to select elements based on the relative position of text strings in various attributes of those elements. Although this section focuses on the `:nth-child()` pseudo-class, you will become familiar with various other CSS3 pseudo-classes, and in the event that you need to use those pseudo-classes, a link is provided at the end of this section which contains more information and examples that illustrate how to use them.

CSS3 supports an extensive and rich set of pseudo-classes, including `nth-child()`, along with some of its semantically related "variants," such as `nth-of-type()`, `nth-first-of-type()`, `nth-last-of-type()`, and `nth-last-child()`.

CSS3 also supports Boolean selectors (which are also pseudo-classes) such as empty, enabled, disabled, and checked, which are very useful for Form-related HTML elements. One other pseudo-class is not(), which returns a set of elements that do not match the selection criteria.

CSS3 uses the meta-characters ^, $, and * (followed by the = symbol) in order to match an initial, terminal, or arbitrary position for a text string. If you are familiar with the Unix utilities grep and sed, as well as the vi text editor, then these meta-characters are very familiar to you.

CSS3 Pseudo-Classes

The CSS3 :nth-child() pseudo-class is both powerful and useful, and it has the following form:

```
:nth-child(insert-a-keyword-or-linear-expression-here)
```

The following list provides various examples of using the nth-child() pseudo-class in order to match various subsets of child elements of an HTML <div> element (which can be substituted by other HTML elements as well):

div:nth-child(1): matches the first child element
div:nth-child(2): matches the second child element
div:nth-child(:even): matches the even child elements
div:nth-child(:odd): matches the odd child elements

The interesting and powerful aspect of the nth-child() pseudo-class is its support for linear expressions of the form an+b, where a is a positive integer and b is a non-negative integer, as shown here (using an HTML5 <div> element):

div:nth-child(3n): matches every third child, starting from position 0
div:nth-child(3n+1): matches every third child, starting from position 1
div:nth-child(3n+2): matches every third child, starting from position 2

CSS3 Attribute Selection

You can specify CSS3 selectors that select HTML elements as well as HTML elements based on the value of an attribute of an HTML element using various regular expressions. For example, the following selector selects img elements whose src attribute starts with the text string Sandra, and then sets the width attribute and the height attribute of the selected img elements to 100px:

```
img[src^="Sandra"] {
  width: 100px; height: 100px;
}
```

The preceding CSS3 selector is useful when you want to set different dimensions to images based on the name of the images (such as `Sandra`, `Shelly`, `Steve`, and so forth).

The following HTML `<img>` elements do not match the preceding selector:

```
<img src="3Sandra" width="200" height="200" />
<img src="Sandra4" width="200" height="200" />
```

The following selector selects HTML img elements whose `src` attribute ends with the text string `jpeg`, and then sets the `width` attribute and the `height` attribute of the selected img elements to `150px`:

```
img[src$="jpeg"] {
  width: 150px; height: 150px;
}
```

The preceding CSS3 selector is useful when you want to set different dimensions to images based on the type of the images (`jpg`, `png`, `jpeg`, and so forth).

The following selector selects HTML img elements whose `src` attribute contains any occurrence of the text string `baby`, and then sets the `width` attribute and the `height` attribute of the selected HTML img elements to `200px`:

```
img[src*="baby"] {
  width: 200px; height: 200px;
}
```

The preceding CSS3 selector is useful when you want to set different dimensions to images based on the "classification" of the images (`mybaby`, `yourbaby`, `babygirl`, `babyboy`, and so forth).

If you want to learn more about patterns (and their descriptions) that you can use in CSS3 selectors, an extensive list is available here:

    http://www.w3.org/TR/css3-selectors.

NOTE   *CSS3 Level 4 selectors enable you to specify the parent of an HTML element. An online tool for converting some CSS3 selector expressions to XPath is here:*
   http://css2xpath.appspot.com.

This concludes part one of this chapter, and the next section delves into CSS3 graphics-oriented effects, such as rounded corners and shadow effects.

CSS3 SHADOW EFFECTS AND ROUNDED CORNERS

CSS3 shadow effects are useful for creating vivid visual effects. You can use shadow effects for text as well as rectangular regions. CSS3 also enables you to easily render rectangles with rounded corners, so you do not need JPG files in order to create this effect.

Specifying Colors with RGB and HSL

Before we delve into the interesting features of CSS3, you need to know how to represent colors. One method is to use (R,G,B) triples, which represent the Red, Green, and Blue components of a color. For instance, the triples (255,0,0), (255,255,0), and (0,0,255) represent the colors Red, Yellow, and Blue. Other ways of specifying the color include: the hexadecimal triples (FF,0,0) and (F,0,0); the decimal triple (100%,0,0); or the string #F00. You can also use (R,G,B,A), where the fourth component specifies the opacity, which is a decimal number from 0 (invisible) to 1 (opaque) inclusive.

However, there is also the HSL (Hue, Saturation, and Luminosity) representation of colors, where the first component is an angle between 0 and 360 (0 degrees is north), and the other two components are percentages between 0 and 100. For instance, (0,100%,50%), (120,100%,50%), and (240,100%,50%) represent the colors Red, Green, and Blue, respectively.

In addition, the HSLa color model supports the alpha/transparency value, which is between 0 (fully transparent) and 1 (fully opaque). The alpha value (in any color model) enables you to "see through" overlapping elements when its value is less than 1, whereas a value of 1 prevents you from seeing the portion of an element that is underneath other elements.

The code samples in this book use (R,G,B) and (R,G,B,A) for representing colors, but you can perform an Internet search to obtain more information regarding HSL.

CSS3 and Text Shadow Effects

A shadow effect for text can make a Web page look more vivid and appealing, and many websites look better with shadow effects that are not overpowering for users (unless you specifically need to do so).

Listing 2.1 displays the contents of the HTML5 page TextShadow1.html that illustrate how to render text with a shadow effect, and Listing 2.2 displays the contents of the CSS stylesheet TextShadow1.css that is referenced in Listing 2.1.

LISTING 2.1 TextShadow1.html

```
<!DOCTYPE html>
<html lang="en">
<head>
  <meta charset="utf-8" />
  <title>CSS Text Shadow Example</title>
  <link href="TextShadow1.css" rel="stylesheet" type="text/css">
</head>

<body>
  <div id="text1">Line One Shadow Effect</div>
  <div id="text2">Line Two Shadow Effect</div>
  <div id="text3">Line Three Vivid Effect</div>
  <div id="text4">
```

```
    <span id="dd">13</span>
    <span id="mm">August</span>
    <span id="yy">2012</span>
  </div>
  <div id="text5">
    <span id="dd">13</span>
    <span id="mm">August</span>
    <span id="yy">2012</span>
  </div>
  <div id="text6">
    <span id="dd">13</span>
    <span id="mm">August</span>
    <span id="yy">2012</span>
  </div>
</body>
</html>
```

The code in Listing 2.1 is straightforward: there is a reference to the CSS stylesheet TextShadow1.css that contains two CSS selectors. One selector specifies how to render the HTML <div> element whose id attribute has value text1, and the other selector matches the HTML <div> element whose id attribute is text2. Although the CSS3 rotate() function is included in this example, we'll defer a more detailed discussion of this function until later in this chapter.

LISTING 2.2 TextShadow1.css

```
#text1 {
   font-size: 24pt;
   text-shadow: 2px 4px 5px #00f;
}

#text2 {
   font-size: 32pt;
   text-shadow: 0px 1px 6px #000,
                4px 5px 6px #f00;
}
/* note the multiple parts in the text-shadow definition */
#text3 {
   font-size: 40pt;
   text-shadow: 0px 1px 6px   #fff,
                2px 4px 4px   #0ff,
                4px 5px 6px   #00f,
                0px 0px 10px #444,
                0px 0px 20px #844,
                0px 0px 30px #a44,
                0px 0px 40px #f44;
}

#text4 {
   position: absolute;
   top: 200px;
   right: 200px;
   font-size: 48pt;
```

```
     text-shadow: 0px 1px 6px   #fff,
                  2px 4px 4px   #0ff,
                  4px 5px 6px   #00f,
                  0px 0px 10px  #000,
                  0px 0px 20px  #448,
                  0px 0px 30px  #a4a,
                  0px 0px 40px  #fff;
     transform: rotate(-90deg);
}

#text5 {
  position: absolute;
  left: 0px;
  font-size: 48pt;
  text-shadow: 2px 4px 5px #00f;
  transform: rotate(-10deg);
}

#text6 {
  float: left;
  font-size: 48pt;
  text-shadow: 2px 4px 5px #f00;
  transform: rotate(-170deg);
}

/* 'transform' is explained later */
#text1:hover, #text2:hover, #text3:hover,
#text4:hover, #text5:hover, #text6:hover {
transform : scale(2) rotate(-45deg);
}
```

The first selector in Listing 2.2 specifies a font-size of 24 and a text-shadow that renders text with a blue background (represented by the hexadecimal value #00f). The attribute text-shadow specifies (from left to right) the x-coordinate, the y-coordinate, the blur radius, and the color of the shadow. The second selector specifies a font-size of 32 and a red shadow background (#f00). The third selector creates a richer visual effect by specifying multiple components in the text-shadow property, which were chosen by experimenting with effects that are possible with different values in the various components.

The final CSS3 selector creates an animation effect whenever users hover over any of the six text strings, and the details of the animation will be deferred until later in this chapter.

Figure 2.1 displays the result of matching the selectors in the CSS stylesheet TextShadow1.css with the HTML <div> elements in the HTML page TextShadow1.html.

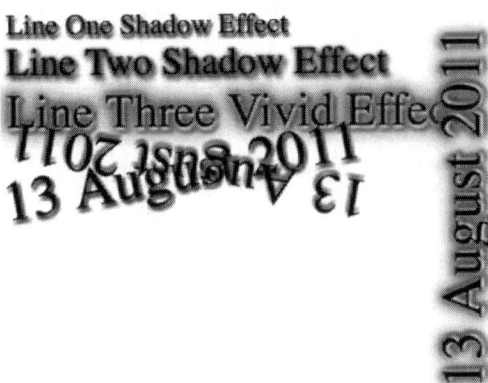

FIGURE 2.1 CSS3 text shadow effects.

CSS3 and Box Shadow Effects

You can also apply a shadow effect to a box that encloses a text string, which can be effective in terms of drawing attention to specific parts of a Web page. However, the same caveat regarding overuse applies to box shadows.

The HTML page `BoxShadow1.html` and `BoxShadow1.css` are not shown here but they are available on the companion disc, and together they render a box shadow effect.

The key property is the `box-shadow` property, as shown here in bold for Mozilla, `WebKit`, and the non-prefixed property:

```
#box1 {
    position:relative;top:10px;
    width: 50%;
    height: 30px;
    font-size: 20px;
    box-shadow: 10px 10px 5px #800;
}
```

Figure 2.2 displays a screenshot based on the code in `BoxShadow1.html` and `BoxShadow1.css`.

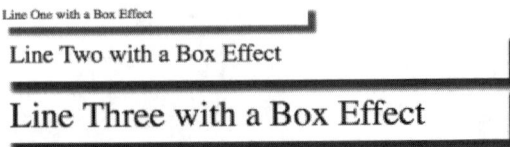

FIGURE 2.2 CSS3 box shadow effect.

CSS3 and Rounded Corners

Web developers have waited a long time for rounded corners in CSS, and CSS3 makes it very easy to render boxes with rounded corners. Listing 2.3 displays the contents of the HTML page `RoundedCorners1.html` that renders text strings in boxes with rounded corners, and Listing 2.4 displays the CSS stylesheet `RoundedCorners1.css`.

LISTING 2.3 RoundedCorners1.html

```
<!DOCTYPE html>
<html lang="en">
<head>
  <link href="RoundedCorners1.css" rel="stylesheet"
    type="text/css">
</head>
<body>
  <div id="outer">
    <a href="#" class="anchor">Text Inside a Rounded
      Rectangle</a>
  </div>
  <div id="text1">Line One of Text with a Shadow Effect</div>
  <div id="text2">Line Two of Text with a Shadow Effect</div>
</body>
</html>
```

Listing 2.3 contains a reference to the CSS stylesheet `RoundedCorners1.css` that contains three CSS selectors that match the elements whose `id` attribute has value `anchor`, `text1`, and `text2`, respectively. The CSS selectors defined in `RoundedCorners1.css` create visual effects, and as you will see, the `hover` pseudo-selector enables you to create animation effects.

LISTING 2.4 RoundedCorners1.css

```
a.anchor:hover {
background: #00F;
}

a.anchor {
background: #FF0;
font-size: 24px;
font-weight: bold;
padding: 4px 4px;
color: rgba(255,0,0,0.8);
text-shadow: 0 1px 1px rgba(0,0,0,0.4);
transition: all 2.0s ease;
border-radius: 8px;
}
```

Listing 2.4 contains the selector `a.anchor:hover` that changes the text color from yellow (`#FF0`) to blue (`#00F`) during a two-second interval whenever users hover over any anchor element with their mouse.

The selector `a.anchor` contains various attributes that specify the dimensions of the box that encloses the text in the `<a>` element, along with two new attributes. The first attribute specifies the `transition` attribute that we will discuss later in this chapter. The second attribute is `border-radius` whose value is `8px`, which determines the radius (in pixels) of the rounded corners of the box that encloses the text in the `<a>` element. The last two selectors are identical to the selectors in Listing 2.1.

Figure 2.3 displays the result of matching the selectors that are defined in the CSS stylesheet `RoundedCorners1.css` with elements in the HTML page `RoundedCorners1.html`.

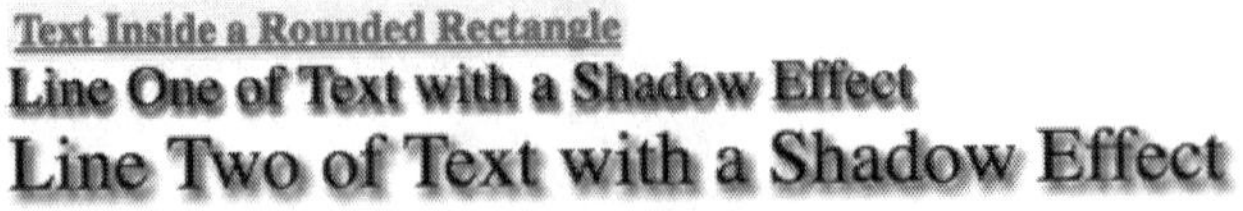

Text Inside a Rounded Rectangle
Line One of Text with a Shadow Effect
Line Two of Text with a Shadow Effect

FIGURE 2.3 CSS3 rounded corners effect.

CSS3 LINEAR GRADIENTS

CSS3 supports linear gradients and radial gradients that create visual effects that are as visually rich as gradients in other technologies such as SVG. The code samples in this section illustrate how to define linear gradients (radial gradients are discussed in the next section) in CSS3 and then match them to HTML elements.

CSS3 linear gradients require one or more "color stops," each of which specifies a start color, an end color, and a rendering pattern. Browsers support the following syntax to define a linear gradient:

- A direction (or an angle)
- One or more color stops

If the `direction` is specified as `to bottom`, the gradient will be rendered horizontally from top to bottom. If the `direction` property is specified as `to right`, the gradient will be rendered vertically from left to right. If the `direction` property is specified as `to bottom right`, the gradient will be rendered diagonally from upper left to lower right.

You can specify an angle instead of the predefined directions: the angle value is the angle between a horizontal line and the gradient line. For example, the following code snippet renders a diagonal linear gradient that forms a thirty-degree angle with the horizontal axis:

```
background: linear-gradient(30deg, red, yellow);
```

The color varies from red to yellow, and is displayed from upper left to lower right.

Listing 2.5 displays the contents of `LinearGradient1.html` and Listing 2.6 displays the contents of `LinearGradient1.css`, which illustrate how to use linear gradients with text strings that are enclosed in <p> elements and an <h3> element.

LISTING 2.5 LinearGradient1.html

```
<!doctype html>
<html lang="en">
<head>
  <meta charset="utf-8" />
```

```
    <title>CSS Linear Gradient Example</title>
    <link href="LinearGradient1.css" rel="stylesheet"
      type="text/css">
</head>

<body>
  <div id="outer">
    <p id="line1">line 1 with a linear gradient</p>
    <p id="line2">line 2 with a linear gradient</p>
    <p id="line3">line 3 with a linear gradient</p>
    <p id="line4">line 4 with a linear gradient</p>
    <p id="outline">line 5 with Shadow Outline</p>
    <h3><a href="#">A Line of Gradient Text</a></h3>
  </div>
</body>
</html>
```

Listing 2.5 contains four <p> elements and one <h3> element. Listing 2.5 also references the CSS stylesheet LinearGradient1.css (displayed in Listing 2.6) that contains CSS selectors that match the four <p> elements and the <h3> element in Listing 2.5.

LISTING 2.6 LinearGradient1.css
```
#line1 {
width: 50%;
font-size: 32px;
background-image: linear-gradient(to bottom, #fff, #f00);
border-radius: 4px;
}


#line2 {
width: 50%;
font-size: 32px;
background-image: linear-gradient(to bottom left, #fff,
#ff0);
border-radius: 4px;
}


#line3 {
width: 50%;
font-size: 32px;
background-image: linear-gradient(to bottom, #f00, #00f);
border-radius: 4px;
}


#line4 {
width: 50%;
font-size: 32px;
background-image: linear-gradient(to bottom left, #f00,
#00f);
border-radius: 4px;
}


#outline {
font-size: 2.0em;
```

```
font-weight: bold;
color: #fff;
text-shadow: 1px 1px 1px rgba(0,0,0,0.5);
}

h3 {
width: 50%;
position: relative;
margin-top: 0;
font-size: 32px;
font-family: helvetica, ariel;
}

h3 a {
position: relative;
color: red;
text-decoration: none;
background-image: linear-gradient(to bottom, #fff, #f00);
}

h3:after {
content:"This is a Line of Text";
color: blue;
}
```

The first selector in Listing 2.6 specifies a font-size of 32 for text and a border-radius of 4 (which renders rounded corners). The *direction* property is to bottom, so the gradient will be rendered horizontally from top to bottom. The linear gradient starts from white #fff and ending with blue #f00, as shown here:

```
#line1 {
width: 50%;
font-size: 32px;
background-image: linear-gradient(to bottom, #fff, #f00);
border-radius: 4px;
}
```

As you can see, the first selector contains two standard attributes. Since the next three selectors in Listing 2.6 are similar to the first selector, we will not discuss their content.

The next CSS selector creates a text outline with a nice shadow effect by rendering the text in white with a thin black shadow, as shown here:

```
color: #fff;
text-shadow: 1px 1px 1px rgba(0,0,0,0.5);
```

The final portion of Listing 2.6 contains three selectors that affect the rendering of the <h3> element and its embedded <a> element: the h3 selector specifies the width and font size; the h3 selector specifies a linear gradient; and the h3:after selector specifies the text string "This is a Line of Text" to display *after* the HTML5 <h3> element (and you can use h3:before to specify a text string to display *before* an HTML5 <h3> element). Other attributes are specified, but these are the main attributes for these selectors.

Figure 2.4 displays the result of matching the selectors in the CSS stylesheet `LinearGradient1.css` to the HTML page `LinearGradient1.html`.

line 1 with a linear gradient

line 2 with a linear gradient

line 3 with a linear gradient

line 4 with a linear gradient

line 5 with Shadow Outline

A Line of Gradient TextThis is a
Line of Text

FIGURE 2.4 CSS3 linear gradient effect.

CSS3 RADIAL GRADIENTS

CSS3 radial gradients are more complex than CSS3 linear gradients, and you can use them to create more complex gradient effects.

A radial gradient requires at least two color stops, and its syntax is here:

```
background: radial-gradient(shape size at position, color1,
..., last-color);
```

The default value for `shape` is `ellipse`; the default value for `size` is `far-thest-corner`; and the default value for `position` is `center`.

A simple example of a radial gradient is here:

```
background: radial-gradient(red, yellow, green);
```

The preceding code snippet renders "evenly spaced" radial gradients, which is the default behavior. An example that specifies offset values for the color stops is here:

```
background: radial-gradient(red 25%, yellow 50%, green 60%);
```

The preceding code snippet renders the color `red` at the position that is `25%` from the beginning of the radial gradient, `yellow` at the halfway point, and `green` at the `60%` position.

The HTML5 Web page `RadialGradient1.html` and the CSS stylesheet `RadialGradient1.css` are not shown here, but the full listing is available on the companion disc. The essence of the code in the HTML5 code involves this code block:

```
<div id="outer">
  <div id="radial3">Text3</div>
  <div id="radial2">Text2</div>
```

```
<div id="radial4">Text4</div>
<div id="radial1">Text1</div>
</div>
```

The CSS stylesheet `RadialGradient1.css` contains five CSS selectors that match the five HTML `<div>` elements, and one of the selectors is shown here:

```
#radial1 {
font-size: 24px;
width:   100px;
height: 100px;
position: absolute; top: 300px; left: 300px;

background: radial-gradient(farthest-side at 60% 55%, red,
    yellow, #400);
}
```

The `#radial1` selector contains a `background` attribute that defines a radial gradient that specifies the farthest-side property, followed by the colors red, yellow, and #400.

The other selectors are simple variations of the first selector that create a slightly contrasting collection of radial gradients.

Figure 2.5 displays the result of matching the selectors in the CSS stylesheet `RadialGradient1.css` to the HTML page `RadialGradient1.html`.

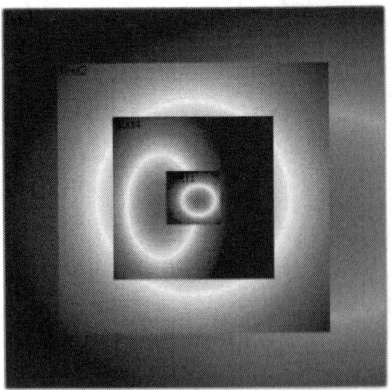

FIGURE 2.5 CSS3 radial gradient effect.

CSS3 GRADIENT GENERATORS

Although you can define CSS3 gradients manually, and even become proficient in doing so, an alternative involves the use of online tools, some of which are listed here:

http://gradientgenerator.com/ and
*https://github.com/istvan-ujjmeszaros/css-gradient-generato*r.
This online CSS3 gradient generator supports Sass:
http://www.colorzilla.com/gradient-editor/.

Experiment with these (and other) CSS3 gradient tools to determine which tools are best suited for your needs. One caveat: some gradient generators will generate code that contains browser-specific prefixes that are no longer required. If you are concerned about generating such code, the following website contains cautionary details regarding gradient generators (specifically about redundant browser-specific prefixes):

http://codepen.io/thebabydino/full/pjxVWp.

CSS3 2D TRANSFORMS

CSS3 supports transforms that you can apply to 2D shapes and also to binary files. The CSS3 transforms are `scale`, `rotate`, `skew` (deprecated), and `translate`, as well as perspective and matrix. Note that you will learn about CSS3 transitions in Chapter 3. However, an alternative is to use GSAP (discussed in Chapter 9) that involves a snippet of SVG (discussed in Chapter 7). For example, consider the following selector:

```
#mytransform {
  /* not supported in IE */
  transform: translateX(100px) scale(0.5);
}
```

Replace the preceding code snippet with the following GSAP transform-related SVG element:

```
<g id="mytransform" transform="matrix(0.5, 0, 0, 0.5, 100,
    0)">...</g>
```

The following sections contain code samples that illustrate how to apply each of these CSS3 transforms to a set of JPG files. The animation effects occur when users hover over any of the PNG files; moreover, you can create "partial" animation effects by moving your mouse quickly between adjacent PNG files. Incidentally, the preceding four transforms are special cases of the CSS3 matrix() function that can specify arbitrary linear 3D transformations, including the CSS3 perspective transform.

Listing 2.7 displays the contents of `Scale1.html` and Listing 2.8 displays the contents of `Scale1.css`, which illustrate how to scale PNG files to create a "hover box" image gallery.

LISTING 2.7 Scale1.html

```
<!DOCTYPE html>
<html lang="en">
<head>
  <meta charset="utf-8" />
  <title>CSS Scale Transform Example</title>
  <link href="Scale1.css" rel="stylesheet" type="text/css">
</head>

<body>
  <header><h1>Hover Over any of the Images:</h1></header>

  <div id="outer">
```

```
        <img src="sample2.png" class="scaled" width="150"
            height="150"/>
        <img src="sample3.png" class="scaled" width="150"
            height="150"/>
        <img src="sample2.png" class="scaled" width="150"
            height="150"/>
        <img src="sample3.png" class="scaled" width="150"
            height="150"/>
    </div>
</body>
</html>
```

Listing 2.7 references the CSS stylesheet Scale1.css (which contains selectors for creating scaled effects) and four HTML <img> elements that reference the PNG files sample2.png and sample3.png. The remainder of Listing 2.7 is straightforward, with simple boilerplate text and HTML elements.

LISTING 2.8 Scale1.css

```
#outer {
  float: left;
  position: relative; top: 50px; left: 50px;
}

img {
  transition: transform 1.0s ease;
}

img.scaled {
  box-shadow: 10px 10px 5px #800;
}

img.scaled:hover {
  transform : scale(2);
}
```

The img selector in Listing 2.8 contains a transition property that applies a transform effect that occurs during a one-second interval using the ease function, as shown here:

```
transition: transform 1.0s ease;
```

Next, the selector img.scaled specifies a box-shadow property that creates a reddish shadow effect (which you saw earlier in this chapter), as shown here:

```
img.scaled {
  box-shadow: 10px 10px 5px #800;
}
```

Finally, the selector img.scaled:hover specifies a transform attribute that uses the scale() function in order to double the size of the associated PNG file whenever users hover over any of the <img> elements with their mouse, as shown here:

```
transform : scale(2);
```

Since the `img` selector specifies a one-second interval using an `ease` function, the scaling effect will last for one second. Experiment with different values for the CSS3 `scale()` function and also different value for the time interval to create the animation effects that suit your needs.

Another point to remember is that you can scale both horizontally and vertically:

```
img {
   transition: transform 1.0s ease;
}

img.mystyle:hover {
   transform : scaleX(1.5) scaleY(0.5);
}
```

Figure 2.6 displays the result of matching the selectors in the CSS stylesheet `Scale1.css` to the HTML page `Scale1.html`.

Hover Over any of the Images:

FIGURE 2.6 CSS3-based scaling effect on JPG files.

Rotate Transforms

The CSS3 `transform` attribute allows you to specify the `rotate()` function in order to create scaling effects, and its syntax looks like this:

```
rotate(someValue);
```

You can replace `someValue` with any number. When `someValue` is positive, the rotation is clockwise; when `someValue` is negative, the rotation is counterclockwise; and when `someValue` is zero, there is no rotation effect. In all cases the initial position for the rotation effect is the positive horizontal axis.

The HTML5 Web page `Rotate1.html` and the CSS stylesheet `Rotate1.css` on the companion disc illustrate how to create rotation effects, a sample of which is shown here:

```
img.imageL:hover {
   transform : scale(2) rotate(-45deg);
}
```

The `img` selector that specifies a `transition` attribute creates an animation effect during a one-second interval using the `ease` timing function, as shown here:

```
transition: transform 1.0s ease;
```

The CSS3 transform attribute allows you to specify the `skew()` function in order to create skewing effects, and its syntax looks like this:

```
skew(xAngle, yAngle);
```

You can replace `xAngle` and `yAngle` with any number. When `xAngle` and `yAngle` are positive, the skew effect is clockwise; when `xAngle` and `yAngle` are negative, the skew effect is counterclockwise; and when `xAngle` and `yAngle` are zero, there is no skew effect. In all cases the initial position for the skew effect is the positive horizontal axis.

The HTML5 Web page `Skew1.html` and the CSS stylesheet `Skew1.css` are on the companion disc, and they illustrate how to create skew effects. The CSS stylesheet containing the `img` selector specifies a `transition` attribute that creates an animation effect during a one-second interval using the `ease` timing function, as shown here:

```
transition: transform 1.0s ease;
```

There are also the four selectors `img.skewed1`, `img.skewed2`, `img.skewed3`, and `img.skewed4`, which create background shadow effects with darker shades of red, yellow, green, and blue, respectively (all of which you have seen in earlier code samples).

The selector `img.skewed1:hover` specifies a transform attribute that performs a skew effect whenever users hover over the first `<img>` element with their mouse, as shown here:

```
transform : scale(2) skew(-10deg, -30deg);
```

The other three CSS3 selectors also use a combination of the CSS functions `skew()` and `scale()` to create distinct visual effects. Notice that the fourth hover selector also sets the `opacity` property to `0.5`, which takes place in parallel with the other effects in this selector.

Figure 2.7 displays the result of matching the selectors in the CSS stylesheet `Skew1.css` to the elements in the HTML page `Skew1.html`.

Hover Over any of the Images:

FIGURE 2.7 CSS3-based skew effects on PNG files.

The CSS3 transform attribute allows you to specify the `translate()` function in order to create an effect that involves a horizontal and/or vertical "shift" of an element, and its syntax looks like this:

```
translate(xDirection, yDirection);
```

The translation is relative to the origin, which is located in the upper-left corner of the screen. Thus, positive values for xDirection and yDirection produce a shift toward the right and a shift downward, respectively, whereas negative values for xDirection and yDirection produce a shift toward the left and a shift upward; zero values for xDirection and yDirection do not cause any translation effect.

The Web page Translate1.html and the CSS stylesheet Translate1. css on the companion disc illustrate how to apply a translation effect to a PNG file.

```
img.trans2:hover {
transform : scale(0.5) translate(-50px, -50px);
}
```

The CSS stylesheet containing the img selector specifies a transform effect during a one-second interval using the ease timing function, as shown here:

```
transition: transform 1.0s ease;
```

The four selectors img.trans1, img.trans2, img.trans3, and img. trans4 create background shadow effects with darker shades of red, yellow, green, and blue, respectively, just as you saw in the previous section.

The selector img.trans1:hover specifies a transform attribute that performs a scale effect and a translation effect whenever users hover over the first <img> element with their mouse, as shown here:

```
transform : scale(2) translate(100px, 50px);
```

Figure 2.8 displays the result of matching the selectors defined in the CSS3 stylesheet Translate1.css to the elements in the HTML page Translate1.html.

Hover Over any of the Images:

FIGURE 2.8 PNG files with CSS3 scale and translate effects.

HOW TO MAKE CSS SELECTORS MORE EFFICIENT

The first part of this section compares two CSS selectors that look very similar, yet they have different results. The second section discusses the trade-offs between using the translate() function versus top/left properties in Web pages.

Browsers read selectors right-to-left: this is a "bottom up" approach, and the "key" selector is the right-most part of a CSS selector. Right-to-left is more efficient because the relationship of element:parent is one-to-one, whereas the relationship of parent:child is many-to-one.

As an illustration, consider the following CSS and HTML fragment:

```
#mylist a { ... }
<ul id="mylist">
  <li a=... class="abc" .../>
  <li a=... class="abc" .../>
  <li a=... class="abc" .../>
....
</ul>
```

Now suppose you have 100 <a> elements, and you want to select the three <a> elements that have a class attribute whose value is abc. This CSS selector matches the complete set of 100 <a> elements (which is not what you want):

```
#mylist a { ... }
```

On the other hand, the following CSS selector matches *only* the three desired elements:

```
#mylist .abc { ... }
```

A sample selector with efficient CSS involving calculate/layout/paint is here:

```
.results h2 {              // recalculate style
   height: 25px;           // layout
   text-shadow: 2px black; // paint
}
```

A slightly older (but still useful) video by Paul Irish about Performance Tooling that covers performance-related topics is here: *http://www.youtube.com/watch?v=HAqjyCH_LOE.*

The translate() Function versus Top/Left Properties

The factors in favor of translate() include that fact that a) translate() does not "touch" the DOM, and b) translate() involves subpixels, which produces smoother effects (partly due to blurring). On the other hand, favor the use of top/left/right/bottom instead of translate() when an element has relative/absolute/fixed positioning in a Web page.

Keep in mind that *both* techniques can yield different results on different browsers. The following detailed articles (by Chris Coyier and by Paul Irish) contain additional information:

http://css-tricks.com/tale-of-animation-performance/ and

http://www.paulirish.com/2012/why-moving-elements-with-translate-is-better-than-posabs-topleft/.

BROWSER-SPECIFIC PREFIXES FOR CSS3 PROPERTIES

Browser-specific prefixes are for CSS properties that are "works in progress" for individual browsers, and the final specification drops browser-specific prefixes. Although more recent versions of modern browsers no longer require prefixes (discussed later in this section), it's worth learning about the prefixes for two reasons: a) you might encounter older code that contains browser-specific prefixes, and b) older websites that generate CSS gradients tend to produce code that contains unnecessary browser-specific prefixes.

The browser-specific prefixes -ie-, -moz-, and -o- are for Internet Explorer, Firefox, and Opera, respectively. Note that Opera also supports -webkit- prefixes, and it's possible that other browsers will do the same (check the respective websites for updates).

As an illustration, the following code block shows examples of these prefixes:

```
-ie-webkit-border-radius: 8px;
-moz-webkit-border-radius: 8px;
-o-webkit-border-radius: 8px;
border-radius: 8px;
```

In your CSS selectors, specify the attributes with browser-specific prefixes before the "generic" attribute, which serves as a default choice in the event that the browser-specific attributes are not selected. The CSS3 code samples in this book contain WebKit-specific prefixes, which helps us keep the CSS stylesheets manageable in terms of size. If you need CSS stylesheets that work on multiple browsers (for current versions as well as older versions), there are essentially two options available. One option involves manually adding the CSS3 code with all the required browser-specific prefixes, which can be tedious to maintain and also error-prone. Another option is to use CSS toolkits or frameworks (discussed in the next chapter) that can programmatically generate the CSS3 code that contains all browser-specific prefixes.

Finally, an extensive list of browser-prefixed CSS properties is here: *http://peter.sh/experiments/vendor-prefixed-css-property-overview/*.

In the case of color gradients (discussed in Chapter 3), you no longer need a browser-specific prefix for the latest versions of Chrome, Firefox, IE 10+, Opera, and Safari. Additional CSS properties will become "prefix free" as modern browsers evolve in terms of feature support. Fortunately, the following open source project enables you to specify prefix-free properties in your code: *http://leaverou.github.io/prefixfree/*.

The preceding code inserts browser-specific prefixes only when it's necessary to do so, which alleviates the tediousness of performing this task manually.

SUMMARY

In this chapter, you learned about browser support for CSS3, browser-specific prefixes, and various CSS3 features. Next you learned about CSS3 pseudo-classes, and how to create shadow effects and rounded corners. You also learned about CSS3 linear and radial gradients as well as online gradient generators. In addition, you saw how to use various CSS3 transforms, such as scale, rotate, skew, and translate. Finally, you learned about performance-related techniques.

CHAPTER 3

CSS3 2D GRAPHICS AND ANIMATION

The previous chapter contains examples of creating CSS3 2D graphics effects, and this chapter contains CSS3 2D animation effects. Note that Chapter 4 shows you how to create CSS3 3D graphics and animation effects. Although CSS3-related graphics and animation effects are discussed in three chapters, please keep in mind that the code samples serve as an introduction to concepts rather than a full and detailed coverage of the technical concepts and features.

The first part of this chapter discusses CSS3 transitions for creating simple animation effects (such as glow effects and bouncing effects). This part of the chapter also contains code samples that show you how to define CSS3 selectors that perform more sophisticated effects with text, such as rendering multicolumn text.

The second part of this chapter shows you how to define CSS3 selectors to create 2D animation effects. Specifically, you will learn how to use CSS3 `keyframes` and the CSS3 functions `scale()`, `rotate()`, and `translate()`, which enable you to create 2D animation effects.

The third part of the chapter shows you how to create fading images, rotating images, and "bouncing" effects. This section also explains how to create CSS3 effects for text (such as multicolumn text). This section also introduces CSS Motion Paths, which is an experimental CSS3 feature that supports SVG-like animation effects. The fourth part of this chapter covers CSS3 filters, along with links to websites that can programmatically generate custom filters for Web pages.

The final section involves jQuery, and how to create 2D effects with jQuery and CSS3. You will also learn how to create a "follow the mouse" example using jQuery and CSS3. If you are unfamiliar with jQuery, you can read the jQuery Appendix that is on the companion disc. You can treat this section of the chapter

ON THE CD

as optional if you do not need jQuery (and perhaps return to this section at some point in the future).

In case you do not already know, there are several advantages to using CSS3 in your HTML5 Web pages. First, you will learn how to create your own visual effects using CSS3 3D. Second, toolkits such as jQuery Mobile rely heavily on CSS3 for rendering content and for creating animation effects (including page transitions). Hence, the knowledge that you gain from the CSS3-related chapters in this book will give you a foundation that will help you understand how jQuery Mobile performs its "magic," and perhaps even also make it easier for you to read the jQuery Mobile source code.

Fourth, it's easier to create very impressive CSS3-based graphics and animation effects (especially in 3D) than to create the same effects in other languages (including SVG). Fifth, your code is likelier to be more compact if you use CSS3 instead of relying on JavaScript and JPG files for graphics and animation, which is a particularly important point for mobile devices. Note that hardware acceleration is mandatory for many CSS3 3D effects, and the good news is that an increasing number of mobile devices support hardware acceleration for CSS3 (and in some cases, there is also such support for HTML5 `Canvas`).

CSS3 2D TRANSFORMS

CSS3 transforms include the CSS3 functions `scale()`, `rotate()`, `skew()`, and `translate()`, which enable you to modify the shape of HTML elements.

This section shows you how to create a cube using CSS3, which involves rendering the front face (a rectangle), the top face (a parallelogram), and the right face (also a parallelogram).

We will use the following CSS3 transforms and effects in this section:

1. The CSS3 `skew()` function to create the left and right faces
2. The CSS3 `scale()` and `rotate()` functions to create the top face
3. Linear and radial gradients for shading effects

The example in this section contains a lot of CSS3 code, and it's probably helpful to launch the Web page in a browser to view the result as you study the code.

Listing 3.1 displays the contents of `3DCube1.html` and Listing 3.2 displays the contents of `3DCube1.css`, which illustrate how to simulate a cube in CSS3.

LISTING 3.1 3DCube1.html

```
<!DOCTYPE html>
<html lang="en">
<head>
<title>CSS 3D Cube Example</title>
  <meta charset="utf-8" />
    <link href="3DCSS1.css" rel="stylesheet" type="text/css">
```

```
</head>

<body>
  <header>
   <h1>Hover Over the Cube Faces:</h1>
  </header>

 <div id="outer">
  <div id="top">Text1</div>
  <div id="left">Text2</div>
  <div id="right">Text3</div>
 </div>
</body>
</html>
```

Listing 3.1 is a straightforward HTML page that references the CSS stylesheet 3DCSS1.css, which contains the CSS3 selectors for styling the HTML <div> elements in this Web page.

LISTING 3.2 3DCube1.css

```
/* size and position */
#right, #left, #top {
position:relative;  padding: 0px;  width: 200px;
  height: 200px;
}
// #left and #right selectors omitted for brevity
```

The transform attribute specifies the CSS3 transform functions scale(), skew(), and rotate(). These three functions are invoked simultaneously, which means that you will see a scaling, skewing, and rotating effect happening at the same time instead of sequentially.

The last three selectors in Listing 3.2 define the properties of each face of the cube. For example, the #left selector specifies the font size for some text and also positional attributes for the left face of the cube. The most complex portion of the #left selector is the value of the background-image attribute, which consists of a combination of a radial gradient, a repeating radial gradient, and another radial gradient. Notice that the left face is a rectangle that is transformed into a parallelogram using this line of code:

```
transform: skew(0deg, -30deg);
```

The #top selector and #right selector contain code that is comparable to the #left selector, and you can experiment with their values in order to create other pleasing visual effects.

Figure 3.1 displays the result of matching the CSS selectors in 3DCube1.css to the <div> elements in the HTML page 3DCube1.html.

If you want to learn how to create various shapes using CSS3 properties and transforms, the following links provide techniques and samples: *http://en-joycss.com/gallery/shapes* and *http://1stwebdesigner.com/css-shapes/*.

FIGURE 3.1 A CSS3-based cube.

CSS3 2D TRANSITIONS

CSS3 transitions involve changes to CSS values in a smooth fashion, and they are initiated by user gestures, such as mouse clicks, focus, or "hover" effects. Transitions are very useful because you can use them to create animation effects on CSS properties for a specific length of time using so-called "easing functions," which produce animation effects at different rates of change. For example, some easing functions vary at a constant rate during an animation effect, whereas others create nonlinear effects (slow-fast-slow, fast-slow-fast, and so forth). Easing functions are powerful and useful because they enable you to create realistic effects, such as watching a baseball moving toward you through the air (this is an example of fast-slow-fast animation).

WebKit originally developed CSS3 transitions, and they are also available in Safari, Chrome (3.2 or higher), Opera (10.5 or higher), and Firefox (4.0 or higher) by using browser-specific prefixes, which you will see later in this section. Keep in mind that there are toolkits (such as jQuery and Prototype) that support transitions effects similar to their CSS3-based counterparts.

The basic syntax for creating a CSS transition is a "triple" that specifies:

- A CSS property
- A duration (in seconds)
- A transition timing function

Here is an example of a transition:

```
transition-property: background;
transition-duration: 0.5s;
transition-timing-function: ease;
```

Fortunately, you can also combine these transitions in one line, as shown here:

```
transition: background 0.5s ease;
```

Here is an example of a CSS3 selector that includes these transitions:

```
a.foo {
padding: 3px 6px;
background: #f00;
transition: background 0.5s ease;
}

a.foo:focus, a.foo:hover {
background: #00f;
}
```

Transitions currently require browser-specific prefixes in order for them to work correctly in all browsers. However, browsers develop quickly, and properties that require a prefix now might become prefix-free in the future. Visit these websites to find out whether or not CSS properties require a prefix: *http://shouldiprefix.com/* and *http://caniuse.com/*.

The following website can help you add browser-specific prefixes for CSS properties: *https://github.com/postcss/autoprefixer*.

Here is an example of specifying a property using browser-specific prefixes for Internet Explorer, Firefox, and Opera:

```
-ie-webkit-transition: background 0.5s ease;
-moz-webkit-transition: background 0.5s ease;
-o-webkit-transition: background 0.5s ease;
```

Currently you can specify one of the following transition timing functions (using browser-specific prefixes):

- Ease
- Ease-in
- Ease-out
- Ease-in-out
- Cubic-bezier

If none of these transition functions is sufficient for your needs, you can create custom functions using this online tool: *www.matthewlein.com/ceaser*.

A website that displays a comparison of transition timing functions is here: *http://www.roblaplaca.com/examples/bezierBuilder/*.

You can specify many values for the property `transition-property`, and an extensive list of values is here: *https://developer.mozilla.org/en/CSS/CSS_transitions*.

According to the preceding link, the property `transition-property` is still experimental, and a browser compatibility table is also available in that link.

The following website is a good source of examples of CSS3 and Bezier curve animation effects: *https://medium.com/@EanPlatter/css3-animations-with-a-cubic-bezier-curve-ea06fc20e5c1*.

ANIMATING A CUBE WITH CSS3 TRANSITIONS

The code sample in this section adds hover-based animation effects to the code sample in the previous section. The HTML Web page `3DCube1Hover1.html` is almost identical to the Web page `3DCube1.html`; the lone exception involves a reference to the CSS stylesheet `3DCube1Hover1.css`.

Listing 3.3 displays the contents of `3DCubeHover1.css`, which contains hover-related CSS3 selectors that create an animation effect for the faces of the cube.

LISTING 3.3 3DCube1Hover1.css

```
#right:hover {
transition: transform 3.0s ease;
transform : scale(1.2) skew(-10deg, -30deg) rotate(-45deg);
}

#left:hover {
transition: transform 2.0s ease;
transform : scale(0.8) skew(-10deg, -30deg) rotate(-45deg);
}

#top:hover {
transition: transform 2.0s ease;
transform : scale(0.5) skew(-20deg, -30deg) rotate(45deg);
}
// the rest of the code is the same as 3DCube1.css
```

Now that you have seen how to use CSS3 2D transforms and transitions, the next section discusses CSS3 keyframes for creating animation effects that do not require user interaction.

ANIMATION EFFECTS WITH CSS3 KEYFRAMES

The CSS3-based code samples that you have seen so far involved primarily static visual effects (but you did see how to use the hover pseudo-selector to create an animation effect). The CSS3 code samples in this section illustrate how to create "glowing" effects and "bouncing" effects for form-based elements.

The CSS3 `@keyframes` rule contains a set of selectors that are identified via a number that represents a percentage between 0 and 100. You also specify the duration of an animation effect on an element, and the duration of each portion of the keyframe is calculated as a percentage of the duration of the effect.

For example, the following CSS3 `@keyframes` rule defines what happens during the first half of the animation as well as the second half of the animation:

```
@keyframes glow {

  0% {
    box-shadow: 0 0 24px rgba(255, 255, 255, 0.5);
  }
```

```
  50% {
    box-shadow: 0 0 24px rgba(255, 0, 0, 0.9);
  }
  100% {
    box-shadow: 0 0 24px rgba(255, 255, 255, 0.5);
  }
}
```

Thus, if the animation effect lasts for ten seconds, then the first two animation effects last for five seconds, followed by the visual effect that is created when the animation effect has completed.

The preceding code block is a simple yet illustrative example that shows you how to use CSS3 @keyframes rules. The example in this section uses keyframes and the hover pseudo-selector in order to create an animation effect whenever users hover with their mouse on a specific element in an HTML page.

Listing 3.3 displays the contents of Transition1.html and Listing 3.4 displays the contents of Transition1.css, which contains CSS3 selectors that create a "glowing" effect on an input field.

LISTING 3.3 Transition1.html

```
<!DOCTYPE html>
<html lang="en">
<head>
  <title>CSS Animation Example</title>
  <meta charset="utf-8" />
  <link href="Transition1.css" rel="stylesheet" type="text/
    css">
</head>

<body>
  <div id="outer">
    <input id="input" type="text" value="This is an input
      line"</input>
  </div>
</body>
</html>
```

Listing 3.3 is a simple HTML page that contains a reference to the CSS stylesheet Transition1.css and one HTML <div> element that contains an <input> field element. As you will see, an animation effect is created when users hover over the <input> element with their mouse.

LISTING 3.4 Transition1.css

```
#outer {
position: relative; top: 20px; left: 20px;
}

@keyframes glow {
  0% {
    box-shadow: 0 0 24px rgba(255, 255, 255, 0.5);
```

```
  }
  50% {
    box-shadow: 0 0 24px rgba(255, 0, 0, 0.9);
  }
  100% {
    box-shadow: 0 0 24px rgba(255, 255, 255, 0.5);
  }
}

#input {
font-size: 24px;
border-radius: 4px;
}

#input:hover {
 animation: glow 2.0s 3 ease;
}
```

Listing 3.4 contains a CSS3 @keyframes rule called glow that specifies three shadow effects. The first shadow effect (which occurs at time 0 of the animation effect) renders a white color with an opacity of 0.5. The second shadow effect (at the midway point of the animation effect) renders a red color with an opacity of 0.9. The third shadow effect (which occurs at the end of the animation effect) is the same as the first animation effect.

The #input selector matches the input field in Transition1.html, which produces a rounded rectangle. The #input:hover selector uses the glow @keyframes rule in order to create an animation effect for a two-second interval, repeated three times, using an ease function, as shown here:

```
animation: glow 2.0s 3 ease;
```

Figure 3.2 displays the result of launching the HTML page Transition1. html. Keep in mind that on desktop browsers you can trigger the animation effect simply by hovering on the input field, whereas on mobile devices you need to tap the input field in order to trigger the animation effect, which will also cause the keyboard to be displayed.

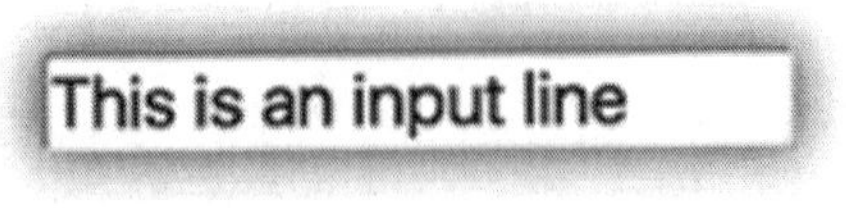

This is an input line

FIGURE 3.2 CSS3 glowing transition effect.

IMAGE FADING AND ROTATING EFFECTS WITH CSS3 KEYFRAMES

The example in the previous section showed you how to create a glowing animation effect, and this section shows you how to create a fading effect with JPG images.

Listing 3.5 displays the contents of FadeRotateImages1.html and Listing 3.6 displays the contents of FadeRotateImages1.css, which illustrate how to create a "fading" effect on a PNG file and a glowing effect on another PNG file.

LISTING 3.5 FadeRotateImages1.html

```
<!DOCTYPE html>
<html lang="en">
<head>
  <title>CSS3 Fade and Rotate Images</title>
  <meta charset="utf-8" />
  <link href="FadingImages1.css" rel="stylesheet"
                                    type="text/css">
</head>

<body>
  <div id="outer">
    <img class="lower" width="250" height="250"
src="sample2.png" />
    <img class="upper" width="250" height="250"
src="sample1.png" />
  </div>

  <div id="third">
    <img width="250" height="250" src="sample1.png" />
  </div>
</body>
```

Listing 3.5 contains a reference to the CSS stylesheet `FadingImages1.css` that contains CSS selectors for creating a fading effect and a glowing effect. The first HTML `<div>` element in Listing 3.5 contains two `<img>` elements; when users hover over the rendered JPG file, it will "fade" and reveal another JPG file. The second HTML `<div>` element contains one `<img>` element, and when users hover over this PNG, a CSS3 selector will rotate the referenced PNG file about the vertical axis.

LISTING 3.6 FadeRotateImages1.css

```
#outer {
 position: absolute; top: 20px; left: 20px;
 margin: 0 auto;
}

#outer img {
 position:absolute; left:0;
 transition: opacity 1s ease-in-out;
}

#outer img.upper:hover {
  opacity:0;
}

#third img {
position: absolute; top: 20px; left: 250px;
}
```

```
#third img:hover {
 animation: rotatey 2.0s 3 ease;
}

@keyframes rotatey {
  0% {
    transform: rotateY(45deg);
  }
  50% {
    transform: rotateY(90deg);
  }
  100% {
    transform: rotateY(0);
  }
}
```

We will skip the code details in Listing 3.6 that are already familiar to you. The key point for creating the fading effect is to set the opacity value to 0 when users hover over the left-most image, and the one line of code in the CSS selector is shown here:

```
#outer img.upper:hover {
  opacity:0;
}
```

As you can see, this code sample shows you that it's possible to create attractive visual effects without complicated code or logic.

Next, Listing 3.6 defines a CSS3 selector that creates a rotation effect about the vertical axis by invoking the CSS3 function `rotateY()` in the `keyframes` labeled `rotatey`. Note that you can create a rotation effect about the other two axes by replacing `rotateY()` with the CSS3 function `rotateX()` or the CSS3 function `rotateZ()`. You can even use these three functions in the same `keyframes` in order to create 3D effects. Note that CSS3 3D effects are discussed in more detail in the next chapter.

Figure 3.3 displays the result of launching `FadeRotateImages1.html`, after tapping on the left image (which is initially the same as the right-side image) that is rendered using a fading effect. Note that on desktop browsers users can hover over either image, and that doing so on the right-side image creates a rotating effect.

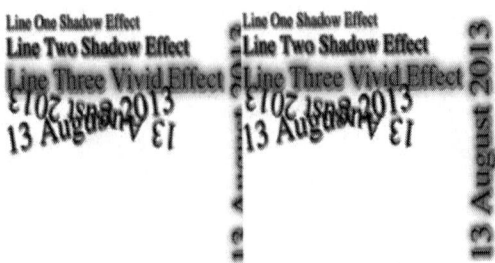

FIGURE 3.3 CSS3 fade and rotate JPG effects.

BOUNCING EFFECTS WITH CSS3 KEYFRAMES

The previous example showed you how to create a fading animation effect, and this section shows you how to create a "bouncing" animation effect.

Listing 3.7 displays the contents of Bounce2.html and Listing 3.8 displays the contents of Bounce2.css, which illustrate how to create a "bouncing" effect on an input field.

LISTING 3.7 Bounce2.html

```
<!DOCTYPE html>
<html lang="en">
<head>
  <title>CSS Animation Example</title>
  <meta charset="utf-8" />
  <link href="Bounce2.css" rel="stylesheet" type="text/css">
</head>

<body>
  <div id="outer">
    <input id="input" type="text" value="An input line"/ >
  </div>
</body>
</html>
```

Listing 3.7 is another straightforward HTML page that contains a reference to the CSS stylesheet Bounce2.css and one HTML <div> element that contains an <input> field element. The CSS stylesheet creates a bouncing animation effect when users hover over the <input> element with their mouse.

LISTING 3.8 Bounce2.css

```
#outer {
position: relative; top: 50px; left: 100px;
}

@keyframes bounce {
  0% {
    left: 50px;
    top: 100px;
    background-color: #ff0000;
  }
  25% {
    left: 100px;
    top: 150px;
    background-color: #ffff00;
  }
  50% {
    left: 50px;
    top: 200px;
    background-color: #00ff00;
  }
  75% {
    left: 0px;
    top: 150px;
```

```
      background-color: #0000ff;
    }
    100% {
      left: 50px;
      top: 100px;
      background-color: #ff0000;
    }
}

#input {
font-size: 24px;
border-radius: 4px;
}

#outer:hover {
 animation: bounce 2.0s 4 ease;
}
```

Listing 3.8 contains a @keyframes rule labeled bounce that specifies five time intervals: the 0%, 25%, 50%, 75%, and 100% points of the duration of the animation effect. Each time interval specifies values for the values for the left, top, and background-color of the <input> field. Despite the simplicity of this @keyframes rule, it creates a pleasing animation effect.

The #input selector matches the input field in Bounce2.html and that results in a rounded rectangle. The #input:hover selector uses bounce keyframes in order to create an animation effect for a two-second interval, repeated four times, using an ease function, as shown here:

```
animation: bounce 2.0s 4 ease;
```

Figure 3.4 displays a snapshot of the animation effect in the HTML Web page Bounce2.html.

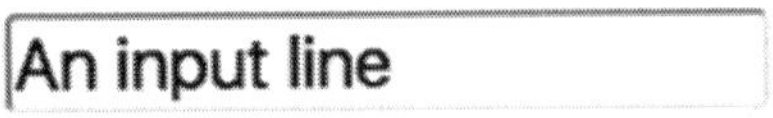

FIGURE 3.4 CSS3 bouncing animation effect.

In addition to CSS3 keyframes, you can use CSS Motion Paths in order to create animation effects, as discussed in the next section.

CSS MOTION PATHS

CSS Motion Paths are currently under development, and they offer tremendous potential in terms of creating complex animation effects in pure CSS3. CSS Motion Paths allow authors to animate any graphical object along an author-specified path. You define a CSS Motion Path in a CSS selector by specifying the motion-path property, whose value involves an actual path in the path() function. CSS Motion Paths support four properties: motion (a shorthand for motion-path), motion-offset (a position on a motion-path), motion-path (an SVG-like path for animation), and motion-rotation (the direction of an element on a motion path).

CSS Motion Paths enable you to create animation effects that are similar to SVG animation effects that have been available since the early days of SVG. In fact, the value for the motion-path property uses an SVG-based syntax, as you can see in the following example:

```
#mydiv {
  motion-path: path('M900,190  L993,245 V201  A11,11 0 0,1
  1004,190  H1075  A11,11 0 0,1 1086,201  V300  L1294,423
  H1216  A11,11 0 0,0 1205,434  V789  A11,11 0 0,1 1194,800
  H606  A11,11 0 0,1 595,789  V434  A11,11 0 0,0 584,423
  H506 L900,190');
}
```

If you are comfortable with SVG, the code in the preceding CSS selector will be very familiar. If you are new to SVG, read the SVG-related material in Chapter 7.

Currently, CSS Motion Paths are supported in some versions of Chrome and Opera (*http://caniuse.com/#feat=css-motion-paths*).

A more extensive example of CSS Motion Paths (involving line segments and elliptic arcs) can be found at *https://googlechrome.github.io/samples/css-motion-path/index.html* and *http://thenewcode.com/38/Animate-Elements-on-a-Path-with-CSS*.

See the complete details regarding the CSS Motion Path specification at *https://drafts.fxtf.org/motion-1/*.

CSS3 EFFECTS WITH TEXT

You have seen examples of rendering text strings as part of several code samples in the previous chapter (and in `TextShadow1.html` in particular), and in this section we discuss a very nice new feature of CSS3 that enables you to render text in multiple columns.

Rendering Multicolumn Text

In Chapter 2, you learned that CSS3 supports multicolumn text, which can create a very nice visual effect when a Web page contains significant amounts of text.

Listing 3.9 displays the contents of `MultiColumns1.html` and Listing 3.10 displays the contents of `MultiColumns1.css`, which illustrate how to render multicolumn text.

LISTING 3.9 MultiColumns1.html

```
<!doctype html>
<html lang="en">
<head>
  <title>CSS Multi Columns Example</title>
  <meta charset="utf-8" />
  <link href="MultiColumns.css" rel="stylesheet"
type="text/css">
</head>
```

```
<body>
  <header>
   <h1>Hover Over the Multi-Column Text:</h1>
  </header>

  <div id="outer">
   <p id="line1">.</p>
   <article>
     <div id="columns">
       <p> CSS enables you to define selectors that specify
the style or the manner in which you want to render
elements in an HTML page. CSS helps you modularize your
HTML content and since you can place your CSS definitions in
a separate file, you can also re-use the same CSS definitions
in multiple HTML files.
       </p>
       <p> Moreover, CSS also enables you to simplify the
updates that you need to make to elements in HTML pages.
For example, suppose that multiple HTML table elements use
a CSS rule that specifies the color red. If you later need
to change the color to blue, you can effect such a change
simply by making one change (i.e., changing red to blue) in
one CSS rule.
       </p>
       <p> Without a CSS rule, you would be forced to
manually update the color attribute in every HTML table
element that is affected, which is error-prone, time-
consuming, and extremely inefficient.
       <p>
       </div>
     </article>
     <p id="line1">.</p>
   </div>
</body>
</html>
```

The HTML5 page in Listing 3.9 contains semantic tags (which are discussed in Chapter 1) that render the text in several HTML <p> elements. As you can see, this HTML5 page is straightforward, and the multicolumn effects are defined in the CSS stylesheet MultiColumns1.css that is displayed in Listing 3.10.

LISTING 3.10 MultiColumn1.css

```
#columns:hover {
transition: transform 3.0s ease;
transform : scale(0.5) skew(-20deg, -30deg) rotate(45deg);
}

#line1:hover {
transition: transform 3.0s ease;

transform : scale(0.5) skew(-20deg, -30deg) rotate(45deg);
background-image: linear-gradient(to bottom, #fff, #00f);
border-radius: 8px;border-radius: 8px;}

#columns {
```

```
column-count : 3;
column-gap : 80px;
column-rule : 1px solid rgb(255,255,255);
}

#line1 {
color: red;
font-size: 24px;
background-image: linear-gradient(to bottom, #fff, #f00);
border-radius: 4px;border-radius: 4px;
}
```

The first two selectors in Listing 3.10 create an animation effect whenever users hover over the `<div>` elements whose id attribute has the value `columns` or `line1`. Both selectors create an animation effect during a three-second interval using the CSS3 functions `scale()`, `skew()`, and `rotate()`, as shown here:

```
transition: transform 3.0s ease;
transform : scale(0.5) skew(-20deg, -30deg) rotate(45deg);
```

The second selector also defines a linear gradient background effect.

The `#columns` selector in Listing 3.10 contains three layout-related attributes. The `column-count` attribute is 3, so the text is displayed in three columns; the `column-gap` attribute is 80px, so there is a space of 80 pixels between adjacent columns; the `column-rule` attribute specifies a white background.

The `#line1` selector specifies a linear gradient that creates a nice visual effect above and below the multicolumn text.

Figure 3.5 displays the result of matching the CSS selectors in `MultiColumns.css` with the text in the HTML page `MultiColumns.html`.

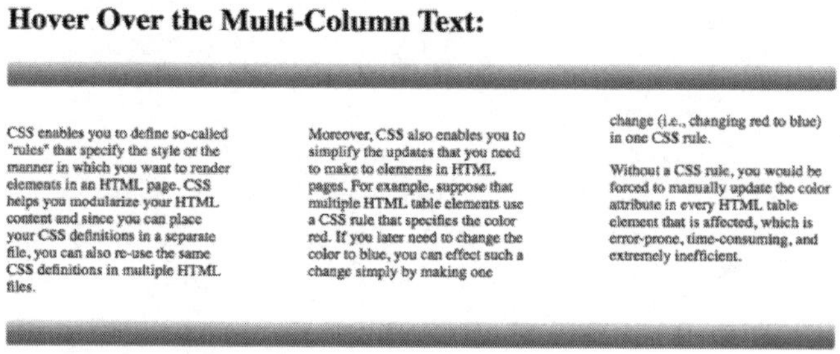

Hover Over the Multi-Column Text:

CSS enables you to define so-called "rules" that specify the style or the manner in which you want to render elements in an HTML page. CSS helps you modularize your HTML content and since you can place your CSS definitions in a separate file, you can also re-use the same CSS definitions in multiple HTML files.

Moreover, CSS also enables you to simplify the updates that you need to make to elements in HTML pages. For example, suppose that multiple HTML table elements use a CSS rule that specifies the color red. If you later need to change the color to blue, you can effect such a change simply by making one

change (i.e., changing red to blue) in one CSS rule.

Without a CSS rule, you would be forced to manually update the color attribute in every HTML table element that is affected, which is error-prone, time-consuming, and extremely inefficient.

FIGURE 3.5 Multicolumn text.

CSS FILTERS

A filter effect is something that you create when you apply a graphical operation on an element in an HTML Web page. Filters can take zero or more input images, and possibly some input parameters. The output image is either displayed in an HTML Web page, or it can be used as the input for yet another filter effect, or provided as a CSS image value.

In addition, modern browsers support the following CSS filters (shown with sample values for each filter):

```
filter: blur(3px);
filter: grayscale(100%);
filter: hue-rotate(80deg);
filter: opacity(0.8);
filter: sepia(80%);
filter: saturate(2);
filter: brightness(0.5);
filter: contrast(0.6 );
filter: hue-rotate(120deg);
filter: invert(0.4);
```

You can apply these CSS filters to JPG files, as shown in the following selector, which styles all the <img> elements with a CSS blur filter:

```
img
{
  filter: blur(3px);
}
```

You can get a complete list of filters and other information from the W3C Editor Draft (which is a work in progress) at *https://dvcs.w3.org/hg/FXTF/raw-file/tip/filters/index.html*.

Two other websites that contain useful information about filters are located at *http://www.ssi-developer.net/css/visual-filters.shtml* and *https://html5-demos.appspot.com/static/css/filters/index.html*.

The Firefox browser provides rich support for CSS filters and developer tools, as can be found at *https://developer.mozilla.org/en-US/docs/Tools/Page_Inspector/How_to/Edit_CSS_filters*.

The following link shows you the status of browser support for CSS filters: *http://caniuse.com/#feat=css-filters*.

CSS Custom Filters

The Adobe website CSS FilterLab enables readers to use point-and-click in order to add CSS filters to a Web page, and also generate the associated code that you can copy/paste into your own HTML Web pages. The CSS FilterLab website is located at *http://www.adobe.com/devnet/html5/articles/css-filterlab.html*.

Keep in mind that there has not been any recent activity on the Github repository for Adobe's CSS FilterLab.

Additional examples of custom filters can be found at *http://www.inserthtml.com/2013/07/css-custom-filters*.

If you are a fan of Instagram, you might be interested in the following toolkit that uses CSS3 to create Instagram filters: *http://una.im/CSSgram/*.

WORKING WITH CSS AND JQUERY (OPTIONAL)

The remainder of this chapter contains examples of Web pages that contain CSS3 and jQuery. You might be asking yourself about the relevance of jQuery in a CSS Pocket Primer. This is a valid question because this *is* a CSS3 Pocket Primer. One option is to simply skip this section (as well as the jQuery sections in other chapters) and perhaps keep these sections in mind in case you decide to learn about combining jQuery and CSS3 at some point in the future.

One other factor to consider is the immense popularity of jQuery, which has led to its inclusion in an incredible number of Web pages. Consequently, the likelihood that you will encounter jQuery code is significant. The purpose of the jQuery code samples is to show you the power of the jQuery `css()` method that greatly simplifies dynamically modifying CSS properties of existing HTML elements as well as creating new HTML elements. Hence, the code samples with jQuery in this chapter only require an understanding of some basic concepts.

The handful of key jQuery concepts for this book are listed here:

1. Use the dollar "`$`" symbol to represent jQuery
2. Locate HTML elements via the syntax `$("name-of-html-tag")`
3. Locate an "`id`" property via the syntax `$("#id-value")`
4. Locate a "`class`" property via the syntax `$("#class-value")`
5. Place your code this block: `$(document).ready(function(){...}`

Here are specific examples:

1. `$("p")` finds all `<p>` elements in an HTML Web page
2. `$("#abc")` finds the HTML element whose `id` attribute has the value "`abc`"
3. `$(".def")` finds the HTML elements whose `class` attribute has the value "`def`"

Listing 3.11 displays the contents of `HelloWorld1.html` that illustrates how to add jQuery functionality to an HTML5 Web page that contains a single HTML `<p>` element.

_____ *Listing 3.11 contains* `console.log()`, *which is available in* `WebKit-`
NOTE *based browsers but might not be available without some type of plugin or extension for other browsers.*

LISTING 3.11 *HelloWorld1.html*

```
<!DOCTYPE html>
<html lang="en">
 <head>
  <meta charset="utf-8" />
  <title>Hello World</title>
```

```
<script src="http://code.jquery.com/jquery-2.0.0b1.js">
</script>
</head>

<body>
 <p id="Steve">Hello World From a Paragraph</p>

 <script>
  $(document).ready(function(){
     // get the 'id' value (which equals Steve)
     var pIdValue = $("p").attr("id");

     // get the text in the <p> element
     var pText = $("p").text();
     console.log (pIdValue+" says "+pText);

     // update the text in the <p> element
     $("p").text("Goodbye World From a Paragraph");
     pText = $("p").text();
     console.log(pIdValue+" says "+pText);
  });
 </script>
 </body>
</html>
```

Listing 3.11 references two jQuery files with this code snippet:

```
<script src="http://code.jquery.com/jquery-2.0.0b1.js">
</script>
```

Notice that the first HTML <script> element in the HTML <body> element starts with this line:

```
$(document).ready(function(){
  // do something here
});
```

The preceding construct ensures that the DOM (Document Object Model) has been loaded into memory, after which it's safe to access and manipulate DOM elements.

Use the jQuery attr() function to get the value of an attribute of an HTML element (such as a <p> element). For example, the following code snippet finds the value of the id attribute of an HTML <p> element:

```
var pIdValue  = $("p").attr('id');
```

Use the jQuery text() function to retrieve the text string in an HTML element. For example, the following code snippet retrieves the text in an HTML <p> element:

```
// get the text in the <p> element
var pText = $("p").text();
console.log (pIdValue+' says '+pText);
```

Finally, you can use the same `text()` function to update the text in an HTML <p> element, as shown here:

```
// update the text in the <p> element
$("p").text("Goodbye World From a Paragraph");
```

Launch the contents of Listing 3.11 in a browser and open the `Inspector` that is available in your browser. Next, select "Inspect Element," and click the ">>" symbol at the bottom of the Web page to see the output from the two `console.log()` statements in Listing 3.11. Keep in mind that the exact sequence of steps for using the Web Inspector in Chrome is different from Safari, and the sequence will probably also change in future versions of these two browsers.

In case you don't already know, you can use `Chrome Web Inspector` to view the contents of variables, which can be very helpful for debugging purposes. You can experiment with the features of `Chrome Web Inspector`, and also read online tutorials about this excellent tool.

2D EFFECTS WITH CSS3 AND JQUERY

If you do not plan to use jQuery in your HTML Web pages, you can treat this section as optional with no loss of continuity.

Listing 3.12 displays the contents of `JQTransforms2D1.html`, which illustrates how to invoke CSS3 2D transforms on <div> elements in an HTML Web page.

LISTING 3.12 JQTransforms2D1.html

```
<!DOCTYPE html>
<html lang="en">
<head>
    <meta charset="utf-8" />
    <title>jQuery and CSS Transforms</title>

    <link href="JQTransforms2D1.css" rel="stylesheet"
        type="text/css">
    <script src="http://code.jquery.com/jquery-2.0.
        0b1.js"></script>
    <script src="http://code.jquery.com/jquery-migrate-
        1.1.0.js"></script>
    </script>
</head>

<body>
  <h1>Click Inside Any of the Rectangles:</h1>
  <div id="outer">
    <div id="inner1"></div>
    <div id="inner2"></div>
    <div id="inner3"></div>
    </div>
  </div>

  <script>
```

```
$(document).ready(function() {
    // one block of code for each <div>

    $("#inner1").click(function() {
      $("div").css({height: '300px',
        'transform': 'scale(0.5, 0.5) skew(-10deg, 20deg)'
      });
    });

    $("#inner2").click(function() {
      $("div").css({height: '200px',
                    width: '250px',
       'transform': 'scale(0.5, 0.8) rotate(-45deg)'
      });
    });

    $("#inner3").click(function() {
      $("div").css({height: '100px',
                    width: '250px',
       'transform': 'skew(-10deg, 10deg) rotate(-45deg)'
      });
    });
  });
  </script>
 </body>
</html>
```

Listing 3.12 contains several <script> elements in the <head> element, followed by the <body> element that contains a <div> element and a <script> element. The <div> element contains three child <div> elements that are matched by selectors in Listing 3.13. The <script> element starts with a jQuery code snippet—shown in bold—that is the standard "check" to ensure the DOM has been loaded into memory. Notice that all the JavaScript and jQuery code is inside this code snippet.

The next portion of Listing 3.12 consist of three blocks of code for handling click events for each of the three nested <div> elements. When users click on any of these <div> elements, the code invokes the jQuery css() method in order to update various properties of the associated <div> element. For example, when users click on the first nested <div> element, the following code block is executed, which applies the scale() function and the skew() function to the <div> element:

```
$("#inner1").click(function() {
    $("div").css({height: '300px',
      'transform': 'scale(0.5, 0.5) skew(-10deg, 20deg)'
    });
});
```

Listing 3.13 displays the contents of JQTransforms2D1.css that contains CSS3 selectors that are referenced in Listing 3.12.

LISTING 3.13 JQTransforms2D1.css

```
#outer {
  position: absolute;
  left: 50px;
  top: 150px;
}

#inner1 {
  float: left;
  background-color:#F00;
  width: 200px;
  height:150px;
}

#inner2 {
  float: left;
  background-color:#FF0;
  width: 200px;
  height:150px;
}

#inner3 {
  float: left;
  background-color:#00F;
  width: 200px;
  height:150px;
}
```

Listing 3.13 contains four CSS selectors that match the four <div> elements in Listing 3.12. The <div> element that matches each selector is updated with values for simple properties whenever users click on the associated <div> element.

Figure 3.6 displays the result of launching JQTransform2D1.html in a Chrome browser.

Click Inside Any of the Rectangles:

FIGURE 3.6 Applying CSS transforms when users click on <div> elements.

"FOLLOW THE MOUSE" WITH CSS3 AND JQUERY

Listing 3.14 displays the contents of JQSketchSolid1.html that illustrates how to invoke CSS3 2D transforms on <div> elements in an HTML Web page.

LISTING 3.14 JQSketchSolid1.html

```html
<!DOCTYPE html>
<html lang="en">
<head>
  <meta charset="utf-8" />
  <title>jQuery Sketching Example</title>

  <script src="http://code.jquery.com/jquery-2.0.0b1.js">
  </script>
  <script
    src="http://code.jquery.com/jquery-migrate-1.1.0.js">
  </script>
</head>

<body>
 <script>
   $(document).ready(function() {
     var render = false; // true/false = draw/no draw
     var shape="", width="8px", height="8px", color="#ff0000";

     $(document).mousedown(function() { render = true; });
     $(document).mouseup(function()   { render = false; });

     $(document).mousemove(function(e) {
         if(render == true) {
            // create a rectangle at the mouse position
            shape = $('<span>').css({'position':'absolute',
                                     'background-
                                        color':color,
                                     'width':width,
                                     'height':height,
                                     top:  e.pageY,
                                        //offsets
                                     left: e.pageX
                                        //offsets
                                    });

            // append rectangle to <body> element
            $(document.body).append(shape);
         }
      });
   });
  </script>
 </body>
</html>
```

Listing 3.14 contains a `<script>` element that defines a JavaScript function for handling `mousedown` and `mouseup` events by toggling the value of the JavaScript variable `render`. The next portion of Listing 3.14 defines the JavaScript function `mousemove` that creates a new `<span>` element and then appends that `<span>` element to the `<body>` element if `render` is `true`, thereby creating a "follow the mouse" effect.

USEFUL LINKS

This section contains an assortment of links with useful additional information for various topics that were discussed in this chapter.

A nice set of "sketch-like" visual effects that use CSS3 is here: *http://andrew-hoyer.com/index.html*.

Compatibility tables for support of HTML5, CSS3, SVG and more in desktop and mobile browsers is here: *http://caniuse.com*.

A website for generating CSS3 code using various CSS3 features is here: *http://CSS3generator.com*.

A website that enables you to perform live editing of the contents of various CSS3 selectors and then see the results is here: *http://CSS3please.com*.

A toolkit that handles the details of browser-specific extensions for CSS3 properties so that you can write prefix-less CSS3 selectors is here: *http://ecsstender.org*.

A website that enables you to create gradients online and view the associated CSS3 code is here: *http://gradients.glrzad.com*.

Another website with information regarding browser support for HTML5 and CSS3 features is here: *http://html5readiness.com*.

An extensive collection of articles regarding HTML5 is available here: *http://www.html5rocks.com/en/*.

A website devoted to all things pertaining to CSS3 is here: *http://www.CSS3.info*.

The following site is an excellent source for browser compatibility information on the Internet (maintained by Peter-Paul Koch): *http://www.quirksmode.org*.

A very good online tool that allows you to experiment with many CSS3 features and also display the associated CSS3 code can be found at *http://www.westciv.com/tools/3Dtransforms/index.html*.

These links provide a wealth of information and useful techniques, so there's a very good chance that you can find the information that you need to create the visual effects that you want for your website.

SUMMARY

This chapter showed you how to create glow and fading effects, and how to render multicolumn text. Then you learned how to use CSS3 `keyframes` and the CSS3 functions `scale()`, `rotate()`, and `translate()`, which enable you to create 2D animation effects. You learned about CSS Motion Paths, which is an experimental CSS3 feature that supports SVG-like animation effects. In addition, you learned about CSS3 filters, along with links to websites that can programmatically generate custom filters for Web pages.

The final section of the chapter delved into combining CSS3 with jQuery in order to create 2D effects, as illustrated in a "follow the mouse" code sample.

CHAPTER 4

CSS3 3D GRAPHICS AND ANIMATION

This chapter shows you how to create HTML Web pages with various 3D graphics and animation effects involving CSS3. However, while 3D effects can be more appealing than 2D effects, they are usually more CPU intensive, which can be problematic for Web pages that are rendered on mobile devices. CSS3 3D effects depend on the GPU (Graphics Processing Unit) to handle intensive computations, and you will learn how to guarantee that the GPU will be invoked. In addition, many Web pages are displayed on mobile devices, so it's important to determine the impact of CSS3 3D animation effects on the battery life of mobile devices.

The first part of this chapter shows you how to use CSS3 2D transforms to render a cube, along with transitions that create an animation effect during hover events. The second part of this chapter discusses 3D transforms, such as translate, scale, and rotate transforms (there is no 3D counterpart for 2D skew transforms). This section also discusses how to create CSS3 transitions.

The third part of this chapter contains examples of 3D animation effects. The fourth part of this chapter shows you how to combine 3D effects with sprites, CSS animation tools, and an optional section that creates animation effects with jQuery and CSS (the jQuery Appendix provides an introduction if you need to familiarize yourself with this technology).

In addition to the code samples that are discussed in this chapter, an extensive set of code samples for creating CSS3 2D/3D graphics/animation effects (mainly for fun) is here: *https://github.com/ocampesato/css3-graphics*.

Since this chapter involves CSS3 3D animation effects, the final portion of this chapter briefly discusses the GPU, its role in HTML, and also shows you how to guarantee that the GPU is invoked for CSS-based animation effects. After you have read the chapters that discuss CSS3 with SVG and CSS3 with HTML5 Canvas, Chapter 9 briefly compares these technologies from the standpoint of performance.

CSS3 3D TRANSFORMS

In general, CSS3 supports 3D transforms that correspond to their 2D counterparts; one exception is the skew transform that does not have a 3D counterpart. Specifically, 3D transforms include: `translate3D`, `rotate3D`, `scale3D`, `matrix3D`, and `perspective`.

Listing 4.1 displays the contents of `3DTransforms.html`, which illustrates how to use CSS3 3D transforms in a Web page, and Listing 4.2 displays the contents of the CSS3 stylesheet `ThreeD2.css`.

LISTING 4.1 Threed2.html

```
<!DOCTYPE html>
<html lang="en">
<head>
  <title>CSS 3D Effects Example</title>
  <meta charset="utf-8" />
  <link href="Threed2.css" rel="stylesheet" type="text/css">
</head>

<body>
  <div id="outer">
    <div id="radial1">Text1</div>
    <div id="radial2">Text2</div>
  </div>
</body>
</html>
```

Listing 4.1 is a simple HTML5 Web page that contains a reference to the CSS3 stylesheet `Threed2.css`, followed by a `<body>` element that contains a `<div>` element whose id attribute has the value `outer`. This same `<div>` element has two child `<div>` elements that match some of the selectors in Listing 4.2.

LISTING 4.2 Threed2.css

```
#outer {
  position: relative; top: 10px; left: 0px;
}

#radial1 {
opacity: 0.8;
font-size: 24px;
width:  200px;
height: 200px;
position: absolute; top: 0px; left: 0px;

background: radial-gradient(
  blue 1%,
  orange 5%, yellow 40%,
  green 60%, red 80%,
  #fff
);

  transform: rotate3d(20,30,40, 50deg)
             translate3d(50px,50px,50px) skew(-15deg,0);
```

```
}

#radial2 {
opacity: 0.6;
font-size: 24px;
width:  200px;
height: 200px;
position: absolute; top: 200px; left: 200px;

background: radial-gradient(
  red 1%,
  orange 5%, yellow 40%,
  green 60%, blue 80%,
  #fff
);

   transform: rotate3d(1,0,0,  60deg) scale3d(1.5, 0.5, 0.75);
}
```

Listing 4.2 contains two CSS selectors, `#radial1` and `#radial2`, that match the `<div>` elements in Listing 4.1 that have corresponding id values. As you can see, these selectors contain the `transform` property that specifies combinations of CSS3 3D functions, such as `rotate3d()` and `translate3d()`, as well as the 2D `skew()` function.

Keep in mind that CSS3 3D transforms might not be supported in all browsers. Check the `caniuse` website for information regarding which browsers support a specific 2D or 3D transform at *http://caniuse.com/#feat=transforms2d* and *http://caniuse.com/#search=css3%203d%20transforms*.

CSS3 3D TRANSITIONS (FIX EXAMPLE)

A CSS transition is an animation effect on a CSS property for a specified duration. The default value for the duration of a CSS transition effect is 0. Hence, a transition will not occur unless you specify the duration of a CSS transition.

Listing 4.3 displays the contents of `3DTransition1.html`, which uses CSS3 transitions that trigger transforms in response to "hover" events.

LISTING 4.3 3DTransition1.html
```
<!DOCTYPE html>
<html>
<head>
  <meta charset="utf-8">
  <title>CSS3 Transition Effect</title>
  <style>
    div {
      width: 150px;
      height: 150px;
      background: red;
      transition: width 2s;
    }
```

```
      div:hover {
        width: 300px;
      }
  </style>
</head>

<body>
  <p>Hover over the following div element:</p>
  <div></div>
</body>
</html>
```

Listing 4.3 contains a `<style>` element that contains a CSS selector that matches HTML `<div>` elements. This selector specifies several CSS properties, including a transition property. The `<style>` element also contains a selector that matches "hover" events over `<div>` elements. In this case, the width of the `<div>` element is increased to 300px. The final portion of Listing 4.3 consists of a `<body>` element that contains a `<p>` element and an empty `<div>` element.

CSS3 supports transitions involving 3D transforms that is analogous to CSS3 2D transitions. You can use the "hover" pseudo-selector in CSS selectors in order detect "hover" events and then perform transitions (and other effects as well).

—————
NOTE *"Hover" events do not occur whenever HTML Web pages are rendered on mobile devices.*

You can specify transition-related timing functions, as shown here:

```
#div1 {transition-timing-function: linear;}
#div2 {transition-timing-function: ease;}
#div3 {transition-timing-function: ease-in;}
#div4 {transition-timing-function: ease-out;}
#div5 {transition-timing-function: ease-in-out;}
```

In addition to the CSS3 property `transition-timing-function`, CSS3 supports transition, transition-delay, transition-duration, and transition-property properties, as described here:

transition: A shorthand property for setting the four transition properties into a single property

transition-delay: Specifies a delay (in seconds) for the transition effect

transition-duration: Specifies how many seconds or milliseconds a transition effect takes to complete

transition-property: Specifies the name of the CSS property the transition effect is for

transition-timing-function: Specifies the speed curve of the transition effect

Browser support for CSS transitions is listed here: *http://caniuse.com/#feat=css-transitions*.

CSS3 3D ANIMATION OF TEXT AND PNG FILES

Listing 4.4 displays the contents of `TextAndImages.html`, which aligns text strings and PNG files, and also creates animation effects when users hover over the text or the PNG files.

LISTING 4.4 TextAndImages.html

```
<!DOCTYPE html>
<html lang="en">
 <head>
  <meta charset="utf-8" />
  <title>Text, Images, and Animation</title>
  <link href="TextAndImages.css" rel="stylesheet"
     type="text/css">
 </head>

 <body>
  <div class="preferences">
    <img src="arrow-up.png"/>
    <p>23 Beer</p>
    <img src="arrow-down.png"/>
    <p>11 Beer</p>
  </div>
 </body>
</html>
```

Listing 4.4 contains a `<div>` element whose class property is `preferences` (which is also a selector in Listing 4.5). This `<div>` element contains two `<img>` elements and two `<p>` elements, both of which are "styled" by selectors in Listing 4.5.

Listing 4.5 displays the contents of the stylesheet `TextAndImages.css`, which contains various selectors that match HTML elements in Listing 4.4.

LISTING 4.5 TextAndImages.css

```
.preferences {
  width: 230px;
  height: 40px;
  background-color:#e2f;
  padding:12px;
  top:20px;
  box-shadow: 0 0 24px rgba(100, 100, 100, 0.9);
}

.preferences > img {
  float:left;
  width: 24px;
  height: 24px;
}

.preferences > p {
  margin:0;
  float:left;
  font-size: 24px;
```

```
      color:red;
      background-color:#48f;
}

p {
   font-size: 24px;
   border-radius: 4px;
   box-shadow: 0 0 24px rgba(100, 100, 100, 0.9);
}

p:hover { scale: 2; animation: rotatex 4.0s 3 ease; }

img { padding:4px; }
img:hover { scale: 2; animation: rotatex 4.0s 3 ease; }

@keyframes rotatex {
   0%    { transform: rotateX(-45deg); }
   25%   { transform: rotateY(90deg); }
   50%   { transform: rotateX(270deg); }
   75%   { transform: rotateZ(135deg); }
   100%  { transform: rotateX(0); }
}
```

Listing 4.5 starts with a selector that matches either the <div> element whose class attribute has the value preferences, or a nested <img> element, or a nested <p> element. The next selector matches the top-level <p> element, followed by a selector that matches when users hover over a top-level <p> element. Similar comments apply to the selector that matches <img> elements and hover events over <img> elements.

The final portion of Listing 4.5 contains a @keyframes definition that specifies (in 25% increments) different degree values in the rotateX() function.

Launch the code in Listing 4.4 and observe the effects that are created.

If you are unfamiliar with the float property (or you need a quick review), the following link is a good read: *http://bitsofco.de/2015/how-floating-works*.

Figure 4.1 displays a screenshot of the animation effect created by hovering over a text string in Listing 4.1.

FIGURE 4.1 Animation effects for text and PNG files.

CSS3 3D ANIMATION EFFECTS WITH KEYFRAMES

In the previous chapter, you learned how to create CSS3 2D animation effects with `keyframes` rules. You can also create CSS3 3D animation effects via CSS3 `keyframes` rules by specifying CSS3 functions, such as `scale3d()`, `rotate3d()`, and `translate3d()`, either individually or in various combinations.

Listing 4.6 displays the contents of `Anim240Flicker3DLGrad4.html`, which is a very simple HTML page that contains four HTML `<div>` elements. The animation effect lasts for four minutes in this example because of the duration that is specified in the associated CSS3 stylesheet.

LISTING 4.6 *Anim240Flicker3DLGrad4.html*

```
<!DOCTYPE html>
<html lang="en">
<head>
  <title>CSS3 Animation Example</title>
  <meta charset="utf-8" />
  <link href="Anim240Flicker3DLGrad4.css" rel="stylesheet"
    type="text/css">
</head>

<body>
 <div id="outer">
  <div id="linear1">Text1</div>
  <div id="linear2">Text2</div>
  <div id="linear3">Text3</div>
  <div id="linear4">Text4</div>
 </div>
</body>
</html>
```

Listing 4.6 is a very simple HTML5 page with corresponding CSS selectors (shown in Listing 4.7). As usual, the real complexity occurs in the CSS selectors that contain the code for creating the animation effects.

As you will see, some of the CSS selectors in Listing 4.6 contain the CSS3 `matrix()` function that requires a knowledge of matrices (which is beyond the scope of this book) to fully understand the reasons for the effects that you can create with the CSS3 `matrix()` function. If you are interested in learning about matrices, you can read this introduction to matrices (in the context of CSS3): *http://www.eleqtriq.com/2010/05/css-3d-matrix-transformations/*.

Since `Anim240Flicker3DLGrad4.css` is such a lengthy code sample, only a portion of the code is displayed in Listing 4.7. However, the complete code is available on the companion disc for this book.

LISTING 4.7 *Anim240Flicker3DLGrad4.css*

```
@keyframes upperLeft {
  0% {
    transform: matrix(1.5, 0.5,  0.0, 1.5, 0, 0)
```

```
                         matrix(1.0, 0.0,  1.0, 1.0, 0, 0);
   }
   10% {
      transform: translate3d(50px,50px,50px)
                 rotate3d(50,50,50,-90deg)
                 skew(-15deg,0) scale3d(1.25, 1.25, 1.25);
   }
   // similar code omitted
   90% {
      transform: matrix(2.0, 0.5,  1.0, 2.0, 0, 0)
                 matrix(1.5, 0.0,  0.5, 2.5, 0, 0);
   }
   95% {
      transform: translate3d(-50px,-50px,-50px)
                 rotate3d(-50,-50,-50, 120deg)
                 skew(135deg,0) scale3d(0.3, 0.4, 0.5);
   }
   96% {
      transform: matrix(0.2, 0.3, -0.5, 0.5, 100, 200)
                 matrix(0.4, 0.5,  0.5, 0.2, 200, 50);
   }
   97% {
      transform: translate3d(50px,-50px,50px)
                 rotate3d(-50,50,-50, 120deg)
                 skew(315deg,0) scale3d(0.5, 0.4, 0.3);
   }
   98% {
      transform: matrix(0.4, 0.5,  0.5, 0.3, 200, 50)
                 matrix(0.3, 0.5, -0.5, 0.4, 50, 150);
   }
   99% {
      transform: translate3d(150px,50px,50px)
                 rotate3d(60,80,100, 240deg)
                 skew(315deg,0) scale3d(1.0, 0.7, 0.3);
   }
   100% {
      transform: matrix(1.0, 0.0,  0.0, 1.0, 0, 0)
                 matrix(1.0, 0.5,  1.0, 1.5, 0, 0);
   }
}
// code omitted for brevity
#linear1 {
font-size: 96px;
text-stroke: 8px blue;
text-shadow: 8px 8px 8px #FF0000;
width:  400px;
height: 250px;

position: relative; top: 0px; left: 0px;

background-image: linear-gradient(#f00,
                                  orange 20%,
                                  yellow 40%,
                                  blue 60%,
                                  green 80%,
                                  #00f);
```

```
border-radius: 4px;
box-shadow:  30px 30px 30px #000;
animation-name: lowerLeft;
animation-duration: 240s;
}
```

Listing 4.7 contains a `keyframes` definition called `upperLeft` that starts with the following line:

```
@keyframes upperLeft {
  // percentage-based definitions go here
}
```

The `#linear` selector contains properties that you have seen already, along with a property that references the `keyframes` identified by `lowerLeft`, and a property that specifies a duration of 240 seconds, as shown here:

```
#linear1 {
  // code omitted for brevity
  animation-name: lowerLeft;
  animation-duration: 240s;
}
```

Now that you know how to reference a `keyframes` definition in a CSS3 selector, let's look at the details of the definition of `lowerLeft`, which contains nineteen elements that specify various animation effects. Each element of `lowerLeft` occurs during a specific stage during the animation. For example, the eighth element in `lowerLeft` specifies the value 50%, which means that it will occur at the halfway point of the animation effect. Since the `#linear` selector contains an `animation-duration` property whose value is 240s (shown in bold in Listing 4.6), this means that the animation will last for four minutes, starting from the point in time when the HTML5 page is launched.

The eighth element of `lowerLeft` specifies a translation, rotation, skew, and scale effect (all of which are in three dimensions), an example of which is shown here:

```
50% {
  transform: translate3d(250px,250px,250px)
             rotate3d(250px,250px,250px,-120deg)
             skew(-65deg,0) scale3d(0.5, 0.5, 0.5);
}
```

The animation effect occurs in a sequential fashion, starting with the translation and finishing with the scale effect, which is also the case for the other elements in `lowerLeft`.

Figure 4.2 displays the initial view of matching the CSS3 selectors defined in the CSS3 stylesheet `Anim240Flicker3DLGrad4.css` with the HTML elements in the HTML page `Anim240Flicker3DLGrad4.html`.

FIGURE 4.2 CSS3 3D animation effects.

CSS3 ANIMATION AND CSS SPRITES

CSS `Sprites` reduce the number of HTTP requests (which reduces response time for Web pages) and also reduce the total file size. The idea is simple: download a single image (which is called a `sprite`) that contains all the smaller images on a website, and then reference the smaller images by their location in the sprite.

This process requires two steps: a) create the sprite, and b) for each image in the sprite, calculate its location in the sprite and then update CSS selectors accordingly. Although you can perform these two steps manually, a much simpler alternative that will save you a lot of time and effort is an excellent tool called `SpriteMe`, which can be found at *http://spriteme.org/*.

This website contains a demonstration that shows you how to install the tool in your bookmarks toolbar and how to easily create a sprite in a matter of minutes for a website. In addition, you can download the generated sprite and the CSS selectors that contain the location of each image that is included in the sprite. After you have created a sprite, you can use the techniques that you learned earlier in this chapter in order to apply 2D and 3D animation effects on your sprite.

Another useful website that contains a collection of techniques and tutorials involving CSS Sprites can be found at

http://namburivk.blogspot.in/2012/05/building-faster-websites-with-css.html?goback=%2Egde_2071438_member_120537762.

The next section discusses performance-related topics, starting with an overview of CSS and the GPU.

HTML WEB PAGES AND THE GPU

The material in this section is admittedly more complex than other sections in this chapter and other chapters in this book, and that's because there are various factors involved to ensure that browsers render graphics smoothly (without any "jank") at many frames per second. Nevertheless, you will see suggestions about the type of CSS code to avoid because of its adverse effect on the performance of a Web page.

As a starting point, browsers render smooth CSS3-based graphics and animation effects with the help of a GPU, which is a single-chip dedicated processor that can improve the performance of video/graphics that involve 2D or 3D graphics.

NOTE *Browsers must be able to use the driver of the graphics card that is installed on the host OS, and GPU acceleration for one browser on a given machine doesn't guarantee support for all browsers.*

Web pages can contain CSS selectors that cause changes in the position of HTML elements. Browsers handle positional changes via two significant operations that can adversely affect performance: repainting and reflow. Repainting involves the calculation of new pixel values (which can be off-loaded to the GPU), and reflow involves calculating the new positions of HTML elements. Note that some CSS-based effects, such as changing the opacity of an element, requires repainting but not reflow if the element does not change its position. Chrome's DevTools provides an "Enable paint flashing" to view the repainting process: when this feature is enabled, green boxes appear around repainted areas. The GPU handles the calculation of pixel values by performing something called "compositing" that involves the creation of one or more "composite layers." These layers are "blended together" in order to combine various effects. You can think of the composite layers as a stack of parallel planes with different colored pixels, and the compositing process as the calculation of the final color of each pixel when the planes are superimposed on each other. The GPU creates a separate composite layer in the following cases: 3D or perspective CSS transforms, `<video>` or `<canvas>` elements, CSS filters, and overlapping elements extracted to a composite layer (such as a z-index).

There is also a size limit in the number of compositing layers that can be created, so it's possible to create animation effects that exhaust the GPU memory. Fortunately, Chrome's DevTools provide a "Show layer border" option that displays each composite layer with an orange border.

One point to keep in mind is that the compositing process is most efficient for changes on elements that can be performed directly in the GPU. Specifically, changes to elements via transform, opacity, or filter can be handled directly by the GPU.

Chrome switches on hardware compositing mode (if supported and not already "on"). Chrome creates a new layer and "backing surface," which is a graphics context (aka texture) into which layers are drawn. Backing surfaces are uploaded to the GPU, and layers sometimes share the same "backing surface." Chrome creates a new backing surface if a layer:

1. Uses 3D or perspective transform CSS properties
2. Is used by a `<video>` element using accelerated video decoding
3. Is used by a `<canvas>` element with a 3D context or accelerated 2D context
4. Uses a CSS animation for its opacity or uses an animated transform
5. Uses accelerated CSS filters
6. Has a descendant that is a compositing layer

7. Has a sibling with a lower z-index which has a compositing layer (is the layer rendered on top of a composited layer?)

CSS Mask and Performance

A CSS Mask results in a new offscreen buffer (OSB). Next, the GPU first writes to the OSB instead of directly to VRAM (Video RAM), after which the OSB contents are copied to VRAM. However, VRAM is comparatively limited on mobile devices and it's "easily exhausted," which can lead to performance degradation. Keep in mind that CSS rounded corners and drop shadows use mask, which is why they can be slow. Moreover, the combination of rounded corners and drop shadows is extra slow.

WHAT ARE REFLOW AND REPAINT?

Reflow is the process of calculating the position of elements in a Web page, whereas Repaint is the re-rendering of pixel colors in a Web page. In CSS, `display:none` causes a reflow and also a repaint because it is neither present nor visible in a Web page. On the other hand, `visibility:hidden` is still present, which means no geometry change, and hence only a repaint is required.

The painting process (browser combines DOM and CSSOM, or CSS Object Model) involves "Skia" for rasterizing software with `Canvas`-like APIs, and the output is a set of bitmaps. Next, the bitmaps are sent to the GPU and the GPU composites them (calculates pixel values). Finally, the GPU renders the output on screen. When you want to change the position of an element, the transform property is more efficient because it's handled directly in the GPU, and no repaint is involved. On the other hand, a combination of the 'left' and 'top' properties causes a reflow as well as a repaint.

Causes of Reflow and Repaint

The following effects result in a reflow and repaint in Web pages:

scroll and hover
box-shadow and drop shadows
floats and tables
opacity and gradients
border-radius
transparency and transitions
changing the font size
leaf-side nodes: probably small changes
top-side nodes: propagation can cause many changes
add/remove/update the DOM

Even "routine" operations that add, remove, or update elements in the DOM will cause a reflow and repaint in a Web page. Thus, it's probably impossible to completely eliminate a reflow and/or repaint in a Web page: the point to keep in mind is that you want to minimize the number of such events so that you do not adversely affect performance and the quality of the user experience on a Web page.

Chrome and Layout Changes

Chrome "batches" layout changes asynchronously in order to maximize rendering performance. The following style information causes synchronous updates:

- OffsetTop and offsetLeft
- OffsetWidth and offsetHeight
- ScrollTop and clientTop
- Left, width, and height
- GetComputedStyle()

The goal is to find and eliminate JavaScript code and/or CSS selectors that cause synchronous updates.

Avoid synchronous updates because any request for style information about a node forces the browser to provide the most up-to-date value. In order to do so, the browser must apply all scheduled changes, flush the queue, and perform a reflow.

For example, minimize this type of code in HTML Web pages:

```
el.style.left = el.offsetLeft + 10 + "px";
```

AUTOMATIC INVOCATION OF THE GPU

When a Web page contains CSS selectors (especially those that involve transforms or animation effects), your browser determines when to invoke the GPU. However, there is no guarantee that the GPU will always be invoked in order to provide improved performance. Fortunately, there are some techniques (sometimes called a "no operation" or "hack") to force the invocation of the GPU. You can use `translate3D(0,0,0)` or `translateZ(0)`, as shown in the following selector:

```
.myelem {
  transform: translateZ(0);
}
```

The following video by Paul Irish (a developer advocate at Google) discusses these and other techniques in this thirty-minute video: *http://paulirish. com/2011/dom-html5-css3-performance/*.

Is it possible that these "hacks" can be slower sometimes? Try this sample code containing 4,000 small <div> elements in your browser: *http:// dl.dropboxusercontent.com/u/17844821/zeug/hwtest.html*.

The following is the original Stack Overflow post (04/2012): *http://stacko-verflow.com/questions/10014461/why-does-enabling-hardware-acceleration-in-css3-slow-down-performance.*

Until recently, Web developers had to rely on the techniques discussed in this section in order to ensure the invocation of the GPU. Starting in 2015, another approach involved the CSS `will-change` property, as discussed in the next section.

The CSS Will-Change Property

The CSS `will-change` property ensures that the GPU is invoked. This property is supported in Chrome 36+, Opera 24+, and Firefox 36+. In addition, Safari is currently implementing `will-change`, and support in Microsoft Edge is "under consideration." More details regarding the `will-change` property can be found here: *http://www.sitepoint.com/introduction-css-will-change-property/* and *https://dev.opera.com/articles/css-will-change-property/.*

DYNAMICALLY CREATING CONTENT WITH JQUERY (OPTIONAL)

This section contains an example of how to dynamically create `<div>` elements and specify matching CSS selectors via the jQuery `css()` method. If you intend to read this section, please also read the introductory jQuery section in Chapter 3 if you are unfamiliar with jQuery. If you intend to skip this section, try launching the code in this section in a browser to see the various effects (you might be surprised).

The purpose of this code sample is two-fold: a) how to create dynamic content via jQuery, and b) how to create animation effects via CSS3 selectors that match the dynamically created content. The code sample in this section will expose you to coding techniques that you can apply to create other CSS3-based animation or graphics effects for your Web pages.

Listing 4.8 displays a portion of the contents of `ArchModEllipsesGrad2.html` that creates CSS3-based 3D animation effects with dynamically created `<div>` elements. The complete code listing is available on the companion disc.

LISTING 4.8 ArchModEllipsesGrad2.html

```
<body>
  <div id="outer"> </div>

  <script>
    var fillColor   = "rgb(255, 0, 0)";
    var basePointX = 300, basePointY = 150;
    var majorAxis = 120, minorAxis = 80;
    var currentX   = 0, currentY = 0;
    var deltaAngle = 3, maxAngle = 720;
    var Constant = 0.25, newNode;
    var rVal = 0, gVal = 0, bVal = 0;
    var stripCount = 10;
    var stripWidth = Math.floor(maxAngle/stripCount);
```

```
$(document).ready(function() {
    for(var angle=0; angle<maxAngle; angle++) {
        radius   = Constant*angle;
        offsetX  = radius*Math.cos(angle*Math.PI/180);
        offsetY  = radius*Math.sin(angle*Math.PI/180);
        currentX = basePointX+offsetX;
        currentY = basePointY-offsetY;

        rVal = Math.floor(255*(angle%stripWidth)/
                            stripWidth);
        fillColor  = "rgb("+rVal+", 0, 0)";

        // create an ellipse at the current position
        if(angle % 20 == 0) {
          newNode = $('<div>').css({
                      'position':'absolute',
                      'width':(angle%majorAxis)+'px',
                      'height':(angle%minorAxis)+'px',
                      left: currentX+'px',
                      top: currentY+'px',
                      'backgroundColor': fillColor,
                      'borderRadius': '20%'
                      }).
                      toggleClass("skewAnim1");
        } else {
          newNode = $('<div>').css({
                      'position':'absolute',
                      'width':majorAxis+'px',
                      'height':minorAxis+'px',
                      left: currentX+'px',
                      top: currentY+'px',
                      'backgroundSize': '240px 240px,
                          80px 80px',
                      'backgroundColor': fillColor,
                      'borderRadius': '50%'
                      }).
                      addClass("radial6 glow");
        }

        $("#outer").append(newNode);
    }
});
</script>
</body>
```

Listing 4.8 consists of a `<body>` element that starts with a `<div>` element whose id attribute has the value "outer." This `<div>` element is where the dynamically created `<div>` elements will be appended, which is performed by the code in the `<script>` element in Listing 4.8.

The `<script>` element initializes some JavaScript variables, and then the standard jQuery "ready" function contains a loop that uses conditional logic to dynamically create `<div>` elements and then append them to the top-level `<div>` element in Listing 4.8.

For example, when the loop variable is a multiple of 20, a new <div> element is created with various CSS attributes, as shown in this code block:

```
newNode = $('<div>').css({'position':'absolute',
                          'width':(angle%majorAxis)+'px',
                          'height':(angle%minorAxis)+'px',
                          left: currentX+'px',
                          top: currentY+'px',
                          'backgroundColor': fillColor,
                          'borderRadius': '20%'
                         }).
             toggleClass("skewAnim1");
```

The "else" portion of the conditional logic dynamically creates another <div> element whose properties are similar.

Figure 4.3 displays the result of launching Listing 4.8 in a Chrome browser.

FIGURE 4.3 Dynamically created <div> elements with jQuery.

If you are interested in other code samples involving jQuery and CSS3 animation effects, an extensive collection of similar code samples (think "swatches") can be found at *https://github.com/ocampesato/jquery-css3-graphics*.

USEFUL LINKS

In addition to Google Chrome, Mozilla Developer Tools has an extensive set of tools for analyzing performance-related bottlenecks in HTML Web pages: *https://www.mozilla.org/en-US/firefox/developer/*.

A nice example of hardware acceleration with CSS animations is here: *http://www.sitepoint.com/introduction-to-hardware-acceleration-css-animations/*.

Many of the CSS3 stylesheets in this book contain selectors with 2D/3D animation effects, and hardware acceleration will significantly improve performance. In fact, some tablet devices do not provide good hardware acceleration, and stylesheets with many 2D or 3D animation effects are almost impossible on those devices.

The following link contains ten items for performance-related CSS3: *http://stackoverflow.com/questions/7486017/css3-what-are-the-performance-best-practices*.

An article that provides information for writing more efficient CSS selectors is here: *http://www.pubnub.com/blog/css3-performance-optimizations*.

Information regarding "best practices" for writing CSS3 selectors is provided here: *http://webdesignerwall.com/trends/css3-examples-and-best-practices* and *http://www.impressivewebs.com/css3-best-practices/*.

A list of tools for CSS animation can be found at *http://speckyboy.com/2015/09/09/css-animation/*.

You can also find other online videos and tutorials regarding CSS3 performance and "best practices" for CSS3 as well as HTML5 Canvas.

SUMMARY

In this chapter, you learned how to create CSS3 3D graphics and animation effects. In particular, you learned about transforms (such as translate, scale, and rotate) and transitions. Then you learned how to create code that invokes the GPU in order to handle intensive computations. In addition, you saw how to combine 3D effects with sprites, and also how to create animation effects with jQuery and CSS.

CHAPTER 5

MEDIA QUERIES AND META TAGS

This chapter is primarily about CSS3 Media Queries, along with coverage of several types of meta tags and discussion of local CSS, which is also provided by Web Components (discussed briefly in Chapter 8). You will learn how to detect screen-related properties (such as width, height, and orientation) of mobile devices using CSS3 Media Queries.

The first part of this chapter discusses CSS3 Media Queries, which enable you to detect some characteristics of a device and render an HTML5 Web page based on those device characteristics. You'll see examples of using CSS3 Media Queries to change the layout of a Web page based on the orientation of a mobile device. CSS3 Media Queries are also used for Responsive Web Design. In Chapter 8, you will learn about Bootstrap, which uses CSS3 Media Queries as a basis for defining different pixel widths (represented by xs, xm, md, and lg) of mobile devices.

The second part of this chapter discusses generic meta tags for mobile devices, along with iOS-specific and Android-specific meta tags. You will also learn how to use "pure" JavaScript in order to detect device orientation (portrait or landscape) and property values (such as the screen width and height) and then update those properties appropriately.

Hence, you can use either CSS3 Media Queries or a combination of CSS3 and JavaScript (or both) in hybrid HTML5 mobile applications. The approach that you adopt probably depends on various factors (project scope and specific requirements) that often involve trade-offs. The spectrum of available techniques, ranging from "pure" JavaScript (more work for you, but a smaller code footprint) to frameworks (larger codebase, but many details are handled for you), affords a range of choices for your HTML5 Web application development.

A quick digression before you read this chapter. In an Appendix, you will learn about preprocessors (such as Sass and LESS) that provide features such as variable definitions. However, preprocessor variables have limitations, some of which affect their usage in CSS3 Media Queries. One possible solution is an interesting feature called CSS Custom Properties (often called CSS variables) that is able to overcome many limitations of preprocessor variables. After you finish the first part of this chapter and the preprocessor-related content in one of the Appendices, consider reading the following articles that introduce you to CSS variables: *https://developer.mozilla.org/en-US/docs/Web/CSS/Using_CSS_variables* and *http://openweb.eu.org/articles/dry-approaches-don-t-repeat-yourself.*

An important caveat: CSS variables are still experimental, with support in Firefox and under development in Chrome. Navigate to this URL for more details about CSS variables: *http://caniuse.com/#feat=css-variables.*

WHAT ARE CSS3 MEDIA QUERIES?

CSS3 Media Queries extend the capability of an older CSS specification known as media types, which assigned browsers to high-level categories such as screen, handheld, or print in order to restyle a Web page's printed output.

CSS 2.1 introduced the concept of media queries, which enable you to conditionally include alternative stylesheets for print, screen, and so forth. The media types specification details ten media types, but browsers only support a few of them (such as screen and print).

For example, the following CSS 2.1 media queries conditionally load CSS stylesheets based on the value of the media attribute:

```
<link rel="stylesheet" type="text/css"
      href="main.css" media="screen" />
<link rel="stylesheet" type="text/css"
      href="print.css" media="print" />
```

The CSS3 Media Queries module extends the idea of media types introduced in CSS 2.1, and all modern desktop and major mobile browsers support CSS3-based media queries.

CSS3 Media Queries give you the ability to determine some of the physical characteristics of a device visiting a site. In a sense, CSS3 Media Queries serve as the counterpart to feature detection. For example, the following CSS3 Media Query combines two conditions as the conditional logic for loading a CSS stylesheet:

```
<link rel="stylesheet"
      media="screen and (min-width: 800px)" href="main.css" />
```

You can also use media queries inline in CSS using @media directives in order to conditionally style various HTML elements, as illustrated in the following example:

```
@media screen and (min-width: 320px) {
   body {
      background-color: #ff0000;
```

```
      }
   }

@media screen and (min-width: 480px) {
   body {
      background-color: #0000ff;
   }
}
```

This section contains an assortment of CSS3 Media Queries, which are very useful logical expressions that enable you detect mobile applications on devices with differing physical attributes and orientation. For example, with CSS3 Media Queries you can change the dimensions and layout of your applications so that they render appropriately on smartphones as well as tablets.

Specifically, you can use CSS3 Media Queries in order to determine the following characteristics of a device:

- Browser window width and height
- Device width and height
- Orientation (landscape or portrait)
- Aspect ratio
- Device aspect ratio
- Resolution

CSS3 Media Queries are Boolean expressions that contain one or more "simple terms" (connected with and or or) that evaluate to true or false. Thus, CSS3 Media Queries represent conditional logic that evaluates to either true or false.

As an example, the following link element loads the CSS stylesheet mystuff.css only if the device is a screen and the maximum width of the device is 480px:

```
<link rel="stylesheet" type="text/css"
      media="screen and (max-device-width: 480px)"
href="mystuff.css"/>
```

The preceding link contains a media attribute that specifies two components: a media type of screen and a query that specifies a max-device-width whose value is 480px. The supported values for media in CSS3 Media Queries are braille, embossed, handheld, print, projection, screen, speech, tty, and tv.

The next CSS3 Media Query checks the media type, the maximum device width, and the resolution of a device:

```
@media screen and (max-device-width: 480px) and
(resolution: 160dpi) {
   #innerDiv {
     float: none;
   }
}
```

If the CSS3 Media Query in the preceding code snippet evaluates to `true`, then the nested CSS selector will match the HTML element whose id attribute has the value `innerDiv`, and its `float` property will be set to none on any device whose maximum screen width is 480px. As you can see, it's possible to create compact CSS3 Media Queries that contain nontrivial logic, which is obviously very useful because CSS3 does not have any `if/then/else` construct that is available in other programming languages.

The following CSS3 Media Query tests the `media` type, the minimum device width, and the resolution of a device:

```
@media screen and (min-device-width: 481px) and
(resolution: 160dpi) {
  #innerDiv {
    float: left;
  }
}
```

In the preceding CSS3 selector, the HTML element whose id attribute has the value `innerDiv` will have a `float` property whose value is left on any device whose minimum screen width is 481px.

The next CSS3 Media Query sets the width of `div` elements to 100px if the screen width is between 321 and 480:

```
@media screen and (min-width: 321px) and (max-width: 480px)
{
    div { width: 100px; }
}
```

In the following code snippet, `myphone.css` would apply to devices that the browser considers "handheld" or devices with a screen width no larger than 320px:

```
<link rel="stylesheet" media="handheld, only screen and
(max-device-width: 320px)" href="myphone.css">
```

NOTE *The use of the "only" keyword in media queries causes non CSS3-compliant browsers to ignore the rule. As another example, the following* `<link>` *loads a CSS stylesheet for screen sizes between* 641px *and* 800px*:*

```
<link rel="stylesheet" media="only screen and (min-width:
641px) and (max-width: 800px)" href="wide.css">
```

Media queries can be included in inline `<style>` tags, as shown in this query, which is for all media types in `portrait` mode:

```
<style> @media only all and (orientation: portrait) { ... }
</style>
```

Now that you have a basic understanding of the sorts of things that you can do with CSS3 Media Queries, you can follow the code in the next section, which contains an HTML5 Web page and a CSS3 stylesheet that illustrate how to handle a change of orientation of a mobile device.

DETECTING SCREEN RESOLUTION WITH CSS3 MEDIA QUERIES

Currently there are few CSS3 Media Queries that are specific to Android devices or iOS devices. Fortunately, you can use CSS3 Media Queries with conditional logic based on different screen sizes or different screen resolutions, some of which are specific to Android devices and iOS devices. You can determine a specific resolution by using the resolution keyword to test for various dots per inch (dpi). You can also specify the min- and max- prefixes to show stylesheets for low-res and high-res machines.

4G iPhone and iPod touches use a high-definition Retina display. You can use a WebKit keyword to test for its presence:

```
-webkit-min-device-pixel-ratio
```

To display only to Retina devices, you would use the following conditional logic:

```
only screen and (-webkit-min-device-pixel-ratio: 2)
```

DETECTING SCREEN ORIENTATION WITH CSS3 MEDIA QUERIES

The CSS3 Media Queries in this section provide a simple example of the capabilities of CSS3 Media Queries.

Listings 5.1 and 5.2 display the contents of the stylesheet CSS3MediaQuery1.css and the HTML5 Web page CSS3MediaQuery1.html, which illustrate how to change the size of two images when users rotate their mobile device.

LISTING 5.1 CSS3MediaQuery1.css

```
@media all and (orientation: portrait) {
  #img1, #img2 {
  float: left;
  width:120px;
  height:300px;
  }
}

@media all and (orientation: landscape) {
  #img1, #img2 {
  float: left;
  width:200px;
  height:200px;
  }
}
```

The code in Listing 5.1 is straightforward: the first selector specifies values for the float, width, and height properties of two PNG files when your mobile device is in `portrait` mode; the second selector specifies different values for the `width` and `height` properties of the two PNG files when your device is in `landscape` mode.

LISTING 5.2 CSS3MediaQuery1.html

```
<!DOCTYPE html>
<html lang="en">
<head>
  <meta charset="utf-8" >
  <title>CSS3 Media Query </title>
  <link href="CSS3MediaQuery1.css" rel="stylesheet"
type="text/css">
</head>

<body>
  <header>
   <h2>Rotate Your Device:</h2>
  </header>

  <div id="outer">
    <div id="one">
      <img id="img1" src="sample2.png" />
    <div>
    <div id="two">
      <img id="img2" src="sample3.png" />
    <div>
  </div>
</body>
</html>
```

Listing 5.2 references the CSS stylesheet `CSS3MediaQuery1.css` in Listing 5.1 in order to apply CSS selectors to the JPG files in the `<body>` element. Next, the HTML `<body>` element contains two HTML `<div>` elements whose `id` attributes have the values `img1` and `img2` that are referenced in the corresponding CSS selectors.

Figure 5.1 displays the result of rendering the HTML page `CSS3MediaQuery.html` in portrait mode on an Android tablet.

Rotate Your Device:

FIGURE 5.1 CSS3 Media Query on an Android tablet.

Figure 5.2 displays the result of rendering the HTML page `CSS3Media-aQuery.html` in landscape mode.

Rotate Your Device:

FIGURE 5.2 CSS3 Media Query on an Android tablet.

DETECTING ORIENTATION WITH SIMPLE JAVASCRIPT

Earlier in this chapter you saw how to use CSS3 Media Queries in order to detect an orientation change of a mobile device. However, keep in mind that it's also possible to do the same thing with simple JavaScript code, so you are not "forced" to use CSS3 Media Queries.

Listing 5.3 displays the contents of the Web page `CSS3OrientationJS1. html`, which illustrates how to use standard JavaScript in order to change the size of two images when users rotate their mobile device.

LISTING 5.3 CSS3OrientationJS1.html

```
<!DOCTYPE html>
<html lang="en">
<head>
  <meta charset="utf-8" >
  <title>CSS3 and Orientation with JS</title>

  <style>
   #img1, #img2 {
      float: left;
      width:120px;height:300px;
   }
  </style>

  <script>
    function init() {
      // Event listener to determine device orientation
      window.onresize = function() { updateOrientation(); }
    }

    function updateOrientation() {
      var orientation = window.orientation;

      switch(orientation) {
        case 0: /* portrait mode */
          document.getElementById("img1").style.width = "120px";
          document.getElementById("img1").style.height = "300px";
```

```
            document.getElementById("img2").style.width  = "120px";
            document.getElementById("img2").style.height = "300px";
               break;

         case 90: /* landscape (screen turned to the left) */
            document.getElementById("img1").style.width  = "200px";
            document.getElementById("img1").style.height = "200px";
            document.getElementById("img2").style.width  = "200px";
            document.getElementById("img2").style.height = "200px";
               break;

         case -90: /* landscape (screen turned to the right) */
            document.getElementById("img1").style.width  = "200px";
            document.getElementById("img1").style.height = "200px";
            document.getElementById("img2").style.width  = "200px";
            document.getElementById("img2").style.height = "200px";
               break;
      }
   }
  </script>
</head>

<body onload="init()">
  <header>
   <h2>Rotate Your Device:</h2>
  </header>

  <div id="outer">
    <div id="one">
      <img id="img1" src="sample2.png" />
    </div>
    <div id="two">
      <img id="img2" src="sample3.png" />
    </div>
  </div>
</body>
</html>
```

As you can see, there is much more code in Listing 5.3 compared to Listing 5.2. In essence, the code uses the value of the variable `window.orientation` in order to detect four different orientations of your mobile device, and in each of those four cases, the dimensions of the PNG files are updated with the following type of code:

```
document.getElementById("img1").style.width  = "120px";
document.getElementById("img1").style.height = "300px";
```

Although this is a very simple example, hopefully this code gives you an appreciation for the capabilities of CSS3 Media Queries.

DETECTING DEVICE ORIENTATION IN 3D USING JAVASCRIPT

The previous section showed you how to determine the orientation of a device in terms of whether it's in portrait mode or landscape mode. In addition, you can determine the position of a device in 3D.

There are three types of changes in the 3D position of a device: up and down (z axis), left and right (y axis), and clockwise and counterclockwise (x axis). These changes are measured with an accelerometer, and you can check their current values in the `deviceorientation` event on the window object. This event fires whenever the mobile device moves, and it returns an object with orientation-related properties.

The JavaScript code looks like the following:

```
window.addEventListener('deviceorientation',function (o) {
  console.log(o.alpha,o.beta,o.gamma);
}, false);
```

The three properties `alpha`, `beta`, and `gamma` provide the rotation angle (in degrees, not radians) in the z, x, and y axes, respectively. Keep in mind that the z axis is the vertical axis (positive is upward), the x axis points toward you (negative is away from you), and the y axis is a left-to-right horizontal axis (toward the right is positive).

The allowable values for these three properties are as follows:

```
alpha: 0 to 360 (clockwise)
beta:  -180 to 180 (toward you/away from you)
gamma: -90 to 90  (left to right)
```

If you want more details regarding the orientation of a device, you can use the accelerometer to obtain more precise information.

DETECTING SCREEN WIDTH AND HEIGHT

The `window` object supports a `resize` event that you can use for determining the width and height of the screen, which in turn enables you to modify other effects in HTML5 Web pages. Listing 5.4 displays the contents of ResizeBorder1.html that illustrates how to maintain the same blue border regardless of the screen size or screen orientation.

LISTING 5.4 ResizeBorder1.html

```
<!DOCTYPE html>
<html lang="en">
<head>
  <meta charset="utf-8" >
  <title>Resizing the Window</title>

  <style>
    * {
      margin:0px; padding:0;
    }

    #outer {
      width: 400px; height: 300px;
      border: 10px solid blue;
    }
  </style>
```

```
    <link rel="stylesheet"
     href="http://code.jquery.com/mobile/1.1.0/jquery.
        mobile-1.1.0.min.css" />
    <script
      src="http://code.jquery.com/jquery-2.0.0b1.js">
    </script>
    <script
      src="http://code.jquery.com/jquery-migrate-1.1.0.js">
    </script>
    <script
 src="http://code.jquery.com/mobile/1.1.0/jquery.mobile-
    1.1.0.min.js">
    </script>
</head>

<body onload="resizeBorder();">
  <div id="outer">
  </div>

  <script>
    // borderWidth equals 'border' in the CSS selector above
    var borderWidth = 10;

    window.onresize = function() { resizeBorder(); }

    function resizeBorder() {
      // do the following if the screen has been resized:
      var rescaledScreenWidth  = document.documentElement.
        clientWidth;
      var rescaledScreenHeight = document.documentElement.
        clientHeight;

      $("#outer").css('width',  rescaledScreenWidth-
        2*borderWidth);
      $("#outer").css('height', rescaledScreenHeight-
        2*borderWidth);
    }
  </script>
</body>
</html>
```

Listing 5.4 contains a `<style>` element whose first selector sets the `padding` and `margin` to `0px` for all elements in the Web page. The second selector specifies a blue border of `10px`. When you load this Web page into a border, and whenever you resize the browser, the JavaScript function `resize-Border()` is executed. This JavaScript function obtains the current width and height of the browser with this code snippet:

```
var rescaledScreenWidth  = document.documentElement.clientWidth;
var rescaledScreenHeight = document.documentElement.clientHeight;
```

The next two lines of code in `resizeBorder()` set the `width` and the `height` properties of the `<div>` element (whose `id` attribute has the value `outer`) equal to the current `width` and `height` values, decreased by the quantity `2*borderWidth`.

CSS3 MEDIA QUERIES FOR MULTIPLE SCREEN SIZES

In the introduction to CSS3 Media Queries you saw examples of defining media queries with compound conditional logic (which can include `and`, `or`, `only`, and `not`). In case you didn't already notice, you can use media queries to handle different screen sizes for mobile devices such as smart phones and tablets. An example of doing so is here:

```
@media screen and (min-width: 321px) and (max-width: 480px)
{
    div { width: 100px; }
}

@media screen and (min-width: 481px) and (max-width: 720px)
{
    div { width: 200px; }
}
```

The logic in the preceding pair of media queries is straightforward: the first media query sets the width of `<div>` elements to `100px` when the screen width is between `321` pixels and `480` pixels; the second media query sets the width of `<div>` elements to `200px` when the screen width is between `481` pixels and `720` pixels.

The following media query sets the width of `<div>` elements to `150px` only when it's a screen:

```
@media only screen {
    div { width: 150px; }
}
```

The following media query sets the width of `<div>` elements to `50px` for devices that do not support orientation:

```
not (orientation)  {
    div { width: 50px; }
}
```

As you can see from the examples in this section and in previous sections, CSS3 Media Queries are simple, flexible, and powerful in terms of their expressiveness and intuitive functionality.

CSS DEVICE ADAPTATION

CSS Device Adaptation enables you to use CSS in order to specify the size, zoom factor, and orientation of the `viewport` meta element in your HTML5 Web pages. As a simple example, the following selector specifies the `width` property and the `zoom` property:

```
@viewport {
  width: device-width;
  zoom: 0.5;
```

```
}
```

You can also embed `@viewport` inside `@media` (using conditional logic that is already familiar to you), as shown in the following example:

```
@media screen and (min-width: 200px) {
  @viewport {
    width: 100px;
  }
}

@media screen and (max-width: 200px) {
  @viewport {
    width: 300px;
  }
}
```

The permissible values for the `viewport` meta element are listed here:

- `width`
- `height`
- `initial-scale`
- `minimum-scale`
- `maximum-scale`
- `user-scalable`
- `target-densityDpi`

More information about CSS Device Adaptation is available in the W3C specification (which is a work in progress): *http://www.w3.org/TR/css-device-adapt/.*

CONDITIONAL LOADING OF ASSETS IN WEB PAGES

Currently there is no recent website with a consolidated list of up-to-date information regarding the use of CSS3 Media Queries to load assets such as images from local directories as well as remote websites (such as CDNs). However, there are links with test-related results and information that might prove useful to you.

An older link with multiple tests pertaining to the downloading of images in CSS3 Media Queries is here: *https://timkadlec.com/2012/04/media-query-asset-downloading-results/.*

The following is a summary of several tests performed in the previous link:

- Hide an image contained in a div by using `display:none`
- A div with a background image that is set to `display:none` if the screen is less than 600px wide
- A `<div>` with a background image is contained in a parent `<div>`, and the latter is set to `display:none` when the screen is less than 600px wide

- A `<div>` with a background image whose color is altered if the screen is less than `600px` wide
- A `<div>` with a background image is given a new background image if the minimum ratio is `1.5` (using the `min-device-pixel-ratio` media query)

Keep in mind that the previous link probably contains some outdated information; however, you can still perform the same tests on your browser of choice to determine whether or not the results are still valid.

Another option involves the use of `window.matchMedia`, which is a JavaScript alternative to CSS3 Media Queries. The `window.matchMedia` APIs are listed here: *https://developer.mozilla.org/en-US/docs/Web/API/Window/matchMedia*.

An article with code samples involving `window.matchMedia` is here: *https://hacks.mozilla.org/2012/06/using-window-matchmedia-to-do-media-queries-in-javascript/*.

The next section of this chapter delves into meta tags, including some that are specific for mobile devices.

THE `VIEWPORT` META TAG

HTML Web pages are rendered in a "virtual page," and the screen is a window into that page. The `viewport meta` tag sets the dimensions of this virtual page. In addition, the `viewport meta` tag controls scaling of the browser window in iOS and Android. The `viewport meta` tag supports the following attributes:

- Width: The width of the viewport in pixels (the default is 980), which can be between 200 and 10,000
- Height: The height of the viewport in pixels. The default is calculated based on the width and the aspect ratio of the device, and it can be between 223 and 10,000
- Initial-scale: the initial "zoom factor" of an application, which users can then scale in and out from that initial value
- Minimum-scale: The minimum scale value of the viewport (the default is 0.25), which can be between 0 and 10.0
- Maximum-scale: The maximum scale value of the viewport (the default is 1.6), which can be between 0 and 10.0
- User-scalable: You can specify whether or not users can zoom in and out in or out of an application (the default is "yes."). Set the value to "no" to prevent scaling

In addition, you can set more than one viewport option in a meta tag by separating them with commas, as shown here:

```
<meta name="viewport" content="width=device-width, user-
    scalable=no">
```

The target-densitydpi property (specified in the viewport meta tag) has been deprecated (and actually removed from WebKit), so it's inadvisable to use this property in order to specify low, medium, or high dpi values in Android-based mobile applications.

You can also use the viewport tag in order to prevent users from zooming or panning in a mobile application. An example is here:

```
<meta name="viewport"
content="width=device-width; initial-scale=1.0; maximum-
scale=1.0; user-scalable=0;" />
```

The iOS platform supports the viewpoint meta tag as well as iOS-specific meta tags, some of which are described here: *http://developer.apple.com/library/safari/documentation/appleapplications/reference/SafariHTMLRef/Articles/MetaTags.html#//apple_ref/doc/uid/TP40008193-SW1.*

Viewport Units

The viewport refers to the browser screen, and the four viewport units are here:

```
vw: the percentage of viewport width
vh: the percentage of viewport height
vmin: the smaller of vw or vh
vmax: the larger of vw or vh
```

For example, 1vw is 1% of the browser's width, which means that 100vw is 100% of the browser width.

The following CSS selector uses the calc() function and a CSS3 Media Query to calculate the font-size property whenever an HTML Web page is resized:

```
html {
  font-size: 100%;

  // Scales by 1px for every 100px (starting from 600px)
  @media (min-width: 600px) {
    font-size: calc(125% + 4 * (100vw - 600px) / 400)
  }

  // Sets font-size to 24px (for 1000px or wider)
  @media (min-width: 1000px) {
    font-size: calc(150%)
  }
}
```

The next portion of this chapter discusses the @import statement for importing a CSS stylesheet into another CSS stylesheet.

THE @IMPORT STATEMENT IN CSS3

The @import statement conveniently enables you to import a CSS stylesheet into another stylesheet. For example, suppose that you want to import the CSS stylesheet `basic.css` into the CSS stylesheet `extended.css`, both of which are in the same directory on the filesystem. You can do so with the following code snippet:

```
@import basic.css
```

You can also import a CSS stylesheet that is available on the Internet instead of the filesystem, as shown here:

```
@import url(http://www.princexml.com/fonts/larabie/index.css)
  all;
```

The next section discusses two important considerations to keep in mind when you use the `@import` statement in CSS stylesheets.

Modularization and Performance

Although the `@import` statement can be very convenient, there are two points to consider when you use the use this statement. First, the `@import` statement can help you modularize your CSS stylesheets, but keep in mind that you need to watch for overriding properties when it's not your intention to do so. Second, there can also be a performance penalty. One popular technique for mitigating the performance degradation is to use a tool that merges files together and then compresses the single concatenated file. This approach reduces the number of HTTP requests and also the total file size that is sent to a Web page.

INLINE AND LOCAL CSS

There are some well-known issues surrounding CSS, such as the global nature of CSS selectors. If you need a refresher about the pros and cons of CSS, including a discussion about inline styles, the following post provides some useful information (along with some interesting reader comments): *https://css-tricks.com/the-debate-around-do-we-even-need-css-anymore/*.

ReactJS supports inline styles "the React way," sometimes also called "CSS in your JS."

The following presentation discusses the problems of CSS and how Facebook has addressed them in ReactJS: *https://speakerdeck.com/vjeux/react-css-in-js*.

The key idea involves converting CSS selectors into JSON-based objects. For instance, suppose you have the following CSS selector:

```
container1 {
  width: 50px;
  height: 50px;
  border-radius:2px;
}

container2 {
  width: 150px;
```

```
  height: 20px;
  border-radius:8px;
}
```

The corresponding JSON object for the preceding CSS selector is shown here:

```
var styles = {
  container1: {
    width: 50,
    height: 50,
    borderRadius:2
  },
  container2: {
    width: 150,
    height: 20,
    borderRadius:8
  }
};
```

In essence, the semicolons are replaced with commas and camel case notation is used for properties that contain a hyphen.

Although React inline styles do solve important problems in CSS, the following blog post ("React Inline Styles Are Fundamentally Flawed") points out the disadvantages of inline styles in React: *https://byjoeybaker.com/react-in-line-styles*.

The preceding link discusses the issues that inline styles introduce regarding vendor prefixes, abstraction, media/element queries, and re-usable animations with @keyframes (among others).

As an example, the following selector definition cannot be converted to a React inline style, which (according to the author) is problematic for iOS because it requires the webkit prefix:

```
div {
  display: -webkit-flex;
  display: flex;
}
```

The author suggests some other toolkits that might be viable solutions:

> *https://github.com/martinandert/react-inline*
> *https://github.com/jsstyles/react-jss*
> *https://github.com/petehunt/jsxstyle*
> *https://github.com/formidablelabs/radium*
> *https://github.com/js-next/react-style*
> *https://github.com/andreypopp/styling*

The following link provides a comparison of CSS in JS libraries for React: *https://github.com/FormidableLabs/radium/tree/master/docs/comparison*.

A second link with a comparison of CSS in JS libraries for React is here: *https://github.com/MicheleBertoli/css-in-js*.

CSS Modules and Local CSS

CSS Modules provides another approach (unrelated to ReactJS) for local CSS via the local-style property. The CSS Modules team provides a namespace-like solution (a previous section describes namespaces), along with separate compilation of different files, in order to provide CSS selectors that are not in the global namespace, and its home page is here: *https://github.com/css-modules*.

The following articles describe CSS Modules in greater depth: http://glen-maddern.com/articles/css-modules and *http://www.sitepoint.com/understanding-css-modules-methodology*.

Web Components and Local CSS

A third approach (also unrelated to ReactJS) is the Shadow DOM that enforces local CSS in different components, which is available in Web Components and Polymer (but not supported in all modern browsers yet).

In Chapter 9, you will learn about Web Components, which enable you to define custom components that contain CSS selectors that are only visible inside the custom component, thereby also providing support for local CSS.

USEFUL LINKS

The following list of links is short yet useful, and each link contains very good information (and you can always perform your own Internet search as well).

The following link contains useful CSS snippets: *http://www.hongkiat.com/blog/css-snippets-for-designers*.

Keep in mind that many of the named snippets (such as box-shadow, text-shadow, border-radius, and opacity) no longer require prefixes, so you can update them accordingly.

A nice set of "sketch-like" visual effects that use CSS3 is here: *http://andrew-hoyer.com/index.html*.

Compatibility tables for support of HTML5, CSS3, SVG and more in desktop and mobile browsers is here: *http://caniuse.com*.

A website for generating CSS3 code using various CSS3 features is here: *http://CSS3generator.com*.

A website that enables you to perform live editing of the contents of various CSS3 selectors and then see the results is here: *http://CSS3please.com*.

A toolkit that handles the details of browser-specific extensions for CSS3 properties so that you can write prefix-less CSS3 selectors is here: *http://ecss-tender.org*.

A website that enables you to create gradients online and view the associated CSS3 code is here: *http://gradients.glrzad.com*.

Another website with information regarding browser support for HTML5 and CSS3 features is here: *http://html5readiness.com*.

An extensive collection of articles regarding HTML5 is available here: *http://www.html5rocks.com/en/*.

A website devoted to all things pertaining to CSS3 is here: *http://www.CSS3.info*.

An excellent source for browser compatibility information on the Internet (maintained by Peter-Paul Koch) can be found at: *http://www.quirksmode.org.*

A very good online tool that allows you to experiment with many CSS3 features and also display the associated CSS3 code is available here: *http://www.westciv.com/tools/3Dtransforms/index.html.*

The following is a website that briefly discusses fourteen CSS generators: *http://www.webpop.com/blog/2013/04/23/css-generators.*

A comparison of fifteen cross-browser testing tools (most are free, and some are commercial) with a tabular comparison of features is here: *http://www.smashingmagazine.com/2011/08/07/a-dozen-cross-browser-testing-tools/.*

These links provide a wealth of information and useful techniques, so there's a very good chance that you can find the information that you need to create the visual effects that you want for your website.

ADDITIONAL CODE SAMPLES

The CSS stylesheet `CSS3MediaQuery1.css` and the HTML5 Web page `CSS3MediaQuery1.html` (both are on the companion disc) illustrate how to use Media Queries in order to change the size of two images when users rotate their mobile device.

You can detect a change of orientation of a mobile device using simple JavaScript code, so you are not "forced" to use CSS3 Media Queries. The HTML5 Web page `CSS3OrientationJS1.html` on the companion disc illustrates how to use standard JavaScript in order to change the size of two images when users rotate their mobile device.

In essence, the code uses the value of the variable `window.orientation` in order to detect four different orientations of your mobile device, and in each of those four cases, the dimensions of the PNG files are updated with the following type of code:

```
document.getElementById("img1").style.width  = "120px";
document.getElementById("img1").style.height = "300px";
```

Although this is a very simple example, hopefully this code gives you an appreciation for the capabilities of CSS3 Media Queries.

SUMMARY

This chapter showed you how to use meta tags in HTML5 Web pages for mobile applications. You saw how to use media queries inline in CSS using `@media` directives in order to conditionally style various HTML elements. You also learned to use CSS3 Media Queries in order to detect an orientation change of a mobile device, as well as accomplishing the same effect using simple JavaScript code. In addition, you learned how to use CSS3 Media Queries with conditional logic based on different screen sizes or different screen resolutions, some of which are specific to Android devices and to iOS devices.

CHAPTER 6

CSS3 AND HTML5 CANVAS

This chapter provides an overview of combining CSS3 with HTML5 Canvas, which is a technology for drawing graphics directly to a part of a Web page. HTML5 Canvas supports various APIs for rendering 2D shapes and creating animation effects. In addition, you will see how to style HTML5 <canvas> elements with CSS3-based animation effects.

You might be wondering why this chapter has been included in this book. If you want to learn about HTML Canvas and the associated JavaScript code, then this chapter will give you a reasonable introduction. There is a second factor for including this chapter: despite the numerous online Canvas-related and CSS3-related tutorials, very few of them combine HTML5 Canvas and CSS3 graphics effects.

The first part of this chapter shows you how to render line segments, rectangles, and circles in HTML5 Canvas, and also how to combine HTML5 Canvas with CSS3 stylesheets. The second part introduces you to linear and radial gradients in HTML5 Canvas, with examples of how to apply them to Bezier curves and binary images. The third part of this chapter contains some examples of rendering PNG files in an HTML Canvas element.

One important caveat: unlike the other chapters in this book, this chapter requires some knowledge of JavaScript, such as how to define variables and functions. In addition, the code samples contain document.getElementById() for finding elements in an HTML Web page, window.addEventListener() for adding an event listener to a Web page, and code for defining click handlers for HTML <input> elements. Admittedly, the details of these methods are not discussed in this chapter. Glance through the code samples to get an idea of the type of JavaScript code that they contain, and then you can assess whether or not you feel confident to read the examples in greater detail. Another suggestion: launch the code samples in this chapter to see which graphics effects interest you, and then you can read the associated code in this chapter.

As you will see, some of the code samples in this chapter contain (sometimes striking) combinations of HTML5 Canvas, CSS3 graphics, and CSS3 2D/3D animation effects that you are unlikely to find in any online resources or topic-related books. These code samples provide a starting point for you to create your own visually compelling graphics effects.

In addition, most of the sections in this chapter start with the syntax of the APIs that are used in the associated code listings, partly because the code samples contain a lot of details and also illustrate multiple concepts. If you want to explore additional HTML5 Canvas graphics after you have finished reading this chapter, an extensive set of code samples is available here: *https://github. com/ocampesato/html5-graphics*.

Keep in mind that it's important to assess the trade-off (time, effort, and cost) between writing low-level Canvas-based graphics code, such as the code samples in this chapter, versus the availability of open source projects and commercial products. If you prefer not to delve into all the JavaScript details for creating HTML5 Canvas effects, there are online drawing tools that can generate the code for you. One free tool that provides some basic functionality is here: *http://www.htmlcanvasstudio.com/*.

WHAT IS HTML5 CANVAS?

Several years ago Canvas began in OS/X as a widget toolkit, and after Canvas had already been available in the Safari browser, it became a specification for the Web, and now it's commonly referred to as HTML5 Canvas.

HTML5 Canvas and SVG both allow you to programmatically render graphics in a browser via JavaScript. However, HTML5 Canvas uses "immediate mode," which is a write-and-forget approach to rendering graphics. Thus, if you want to write a sketching program in HTML5 Canvas and you also want to provide an "undo" feature, then you must programmatically keep track of everything that users have drawn on the screen. On the other hand, SVG uses a "retained mode," which involves a DOM structure that keeps track of the rendered objects and their relationship to one another.

If you are going to write HTML Web pages that make extensive use of graphics effects, you'll probably need to understand the differences between HTML5 Canvas and SVG in terms of performance. You have the freedom to use one technology exclusively, but you can also create HTML Web pages that contain a mixture of HTML5 Canvas, SVG, and CSS3, and performance-related information can help you decide how you are going to code your HTML Web pages.

Although this chapter does not delve into the preceding points in any more detail, you can find a good overview of some features/advantages of HTML5 Canvas here: *http://thinkvitamin.com/code/how-to-draw-with-html-5-canvas/*.

THE HTML5 CANVAS COORDINATE SYSTEM

Think back to your days in high school, where you learned that the Cartesian coordinate system identifies any point in the Euclidean plane by means of a pair of numbers, often written as (x, y). The first number represents the horizontal value and the second number represents the vertical value. The horizontal axis is labeled the x-axis, and positive values on the x-axis are to the right of the vertical axis (i.e., toward the right). The vertical axis is labeled the y-axis, and positive values on the y-axis are above the horizontal axis. The origin is the intersection point of the x-axis and the y-axis.

The situation is almost the same in the HTML5 Canvas coordinate system. The x-axis is horizontal and the positive direction is toward the right. The y-axis is vertical, but the positive direction is *downward*, which is the opposite direction of most graphs in a typical mathematics textbook. In the HTML5 Canvas coordinate system, the origin is the upper-left corner of the screen (not the lower-left corner), and the unit of measurement is the pixel.

As a simple illustration, Figure 6.1 displays four points in an HTML5 <canvas> element.

FIGURE 6.1 Four points rendered in HTML5 Canvas.

If you start from the origin (the upper-left corner of the screen) and move 50 pixels to the right, followed by 50 pixels downward, you will reach the upper-left point in Figure 6.1. Next, if you start from the origin and move 200 pixels to the right and 50 pixels downward, you will reach the upper-right point in Listing 6.1. In a similar fashion, the two points in the second "row" have coordinates (50,100) and (200,100). Notice that the two points in the first row have the same value for the y-coordinate, which makes sense because they are the same distance away from the top of the Web page; the same is true for the two points in the second row. Similarly, the two points in the left "column" have the same x-coordinate because they are both the same distance from the left side of the Web page.

Now that you have an understanding of the HTML5 Canvas coordinate system, let's take a look at the contents of Listing 6.1, which displays a minimal HTML5 Web page that is ready for rendering HTML5 Canvas-based graphics.

The Canvas-based code samples in this chapter contain the code (or some variant) that is displayed in Listing 6.1.

NOTE *If you launch this code in a browser session, you will only see a blank screen.*

LISTING 6.1 Canvas1.html

```html
<!DOCTYPE html>
<html lang="en">
 <head>
  <meta charset="utf-8">
  <title>Canvas Example</title>

  <script><!--
    window.addEventListener('load', function () {
      // Get the canvas element
      var elem = document.getElementById('myCanvas');
      if (!elem || !elem.getContext) {
        return;
      }

      // Get the canvas 2d context
      var context = elem.getContext('2d');
      if (!context) {
        return;
      }

      // Insert your custom Canvas graphics code here
      });
    // --></script>
 </head>

 <body>
  <p>
   <canvas id="myCanvas" width="300" height="300">
                           No support for Canvas.
   </canvas>
  </p>
 </body>
</html>
```

Listing 6.1 contains an HTML <head> element that checks for the existence of an HTML <canvas> element inside the HTML <body> element of the Web page, and then gets the 2D context from the HTML <canvas> element. If you skip over the various conditional statements in Listing 6.1, there are two lines of code that enable us to get a reference to the variable context, which represents a drawable surface:

```
var elem = document.getElementById('myCanvas');
var context = elem.getContext('2d');
```

If you launch Listing 6.1 in a browser that does not support HTML5 Canvas, it will display the text message "No support for Canvas."

The following code snippet is executed whenever you launch the Web page because of an anonymous JavaScript function that is executed during the load event:

```
<script><!--
window.addEventListener('load', function () {
  // do something here
});
// --></script>
```

Now that you understand the underlying code for rendering Canvas-based 2D shapes, you can focus on the code that actually draws some 2D shapes, starting with the example in the next section.

LINE SEGMENTS, RECTANGLES, CIRCLES, AND SHADOW EFFECTS

This section contains an assortment of code samples that illustrate how to render 2D shapes in HTML5 Canvas. There are many concepts introduced in this section, so before delving into the code sample, let's look at some of the HTML5 Canvas APIs that are used in this section. Chapter 2 contains a section that describes various ways for specifying colors, and the material in that section is relevant for the code sample in this chapter (so you can quickly review its contents now if you need to do so).

HTML5 Canvas provides the fillRect() method for rendering a rectangle, which requires four parameters: the upper-left vertex (defined by its x-coordinate and its y-coordinate) of the rectangle, the width of the rectangle, and the height of the desired rectangle. The Canvas fillRect() API looks like this:

```
context.fillRect(x, y, width, height);
```

HTML5 Canvas allows you to render line segments by specifying the (x, y) coordinates of the two endpoints of a line segment. The two new APIs that are used in the code sample in this section are moveTo() and lineTo(), and they look like this:

```
context.moveTo(x1, y1);
context.lineTo(x2, y2);
```

The preceding code snippet represents the line segment whose two endpoints are specified by the points (x1, y1) and (x2, y2). Note that you can also render the same line segment with the following code snippet:

```
context.moveTo(x2, y2);
context.lineTo(x1, y1);
```

Shadow effects provide a richer visual experience that is an improvement over the use of non-shadow effects. You create a shadow effect by assigning values to three shadow-related attributes that control the size of the underlying shadow and also the extent of the "fuzziness" of the shadow, as shown here:

```
context.shadowOffsetX = shadowX;
context.shadowOffsetY = shadowY;
context.shadowBlur    = 4;
```

You can also assign (R,G,B) or (R,G,B,A) values to shadowColor (which is an attribute of the drawing context) as shown here:

```
context.shadowColor   = "rgba(0,0,64,1.0)";
```

The HTML5 Web page RandRectanglesShadow.html in Listing 6.2 uses this technique in order to render a set of randomly generated rectangles with a shadow effect.

LISTING 6.2 RandRectanglesShadow.html

```
<!DOCTYPE html>
<html lang="en">
<head>
  <meta charset="utf-8">
  <title>Canvas Random Rectangles With Shadow Effects</title>
  <link href="CSS3Background2.css" rel="stylesheet"
                                            type="text/css">

  <style>
    input {
      width:300px;
      font-size:24px;
      background-color:#f00;
    }
  </style>

  <script><!--
    window.addEventListener('load', function() {
      var clickCount = 0;

      // Get the canvas element
      var elem = document.getElementById('myCanvas');
      if (!elem || !elem.getContext) {
        return;
      }

      // Get the canvas 2d context
      var context = elem.getContext('2d');
      if (!context) {
        return;
      }

      var basePointX = 10;
      var basePointY = 10;
      var canWidth   = 800;
```

```
        var canHeight  = 450;
        var shadowX    = 10;
        var shadowY    = 10;
        var rectCount  = 100;
        var rectWidth  = 100;
        var rectHeight = 100;
        var colorIndex = 0;
        var fillStyles = ['#f00', '#ff0', '#0f0', '#00f'];

        redrawCanvas = function() {
            // clear the canvas before drawing new set of rectangles
            context.clearRect(0, 0, elem.width, elem.height);

            for(var r=0; r<rectCount; r++) {
                basePointX = canWidth*Math.random();
                basePointY = canHeight*Math.random();

                // Alternate shadow effect based on an even/odd
                // click count with different (R,G,B,A) values
                if(clickCount % 2 == 0) {
                    context.shadowColor   = "rgba(0,0,64,1.0)";
                } else {
                    context.shadowColor   = "rgba(64,0,0,1.0)";
                }

                // code that specifies the size and also the
                // "fuzziness" of the underlying shadow effect
                context.shadowOffsetX = shadowX;
                context.shadowOffsetY = shadowY;
                context.shadowBlur    = 4;
                context.lineWidth     = 1;

                // render a colored rectangle
                colorIndex = Math.floor(basePointX)%fillStyles.length;
                context.fillStyle = fillStyles[colorIndex];

                context.fillRect(basePointX, basePointY,
                                 rectWidth, rectHeight);

                ++clickCount;
            }
        }

        // render a set of random rectangles
        redrawCanvas();
    });
    // --></script>
  </head>

  <body>
    <div>
      <canvas id="myCanvas" width="800" height="450">No support
for Canvas
      </canvas>
    </div>
```

```
<div>
  <input type="button" onclick="redrawCanvas();return false"
        value="Redraw the Rectangles" />
</div>
</body>
</html>
```

The HTML5 code in Listing 6.2 starts by initializing some JavaScript variables and then defining the JavaScript function `redrawCanvas()` that contains a loop for rendering the rectangles on the screen. The loop calculates the coordinates of the upper-left vertex of each rectangle as shown here:

```
basePointX = canWidth*Math.random();
basePointY = canHeight*Math.random();
```

The next part of the loop assigns the background color (which alternates between a dark blue and dark red shadow), and then sets up a shadow effect by specifying values for the attributes `shadowOffsetX`, `shadowOffsetY`, and `shadowBlur`, as shown here:

```
context.shadowOffsetX = shadowX;
context.shadowOffsetY = shadowY;
context.shadowBlur    = 4;
```

The actual rendering of each rectangle is performed by the following code:

```
context.fillRect(basePointX, basePointY,
                 rectWidth, rectHeight);
```

Notice that the `clickCount` variable is incremented each time users click inside the HTML5 `Canvas` element, and its value determines which shadow color is applied to the randomly generated rectangles.

Although shadow effects create a pleasing effect, they also have an impact on performance. If you need shadow-like effects but performance becomes an issue, one alternative is to render a background shape in black (or some other dark color) and then render the same shape (with a small offset) using a different color.

For example, you can create a shadow effect for rectangles by first rendering a black rectangle and then rendering a red rectangle on top of the black rectangle, as shown here:

```
// render a black rectangle
context.fillStyle = '#000';
context.fillRect(50+shadowX, 50+shadowY, 200, 100);

// render a red rectangle
context.fillStyle = '#f00';
context.fillRect(50, 50, 200, 100);
```

The values for `shadowX` and `shadowY` determine the size of the background "shadow," and the choice of positive versus negative values for `shadowX` and shadowY will determine the relative position of the black rectangle with respect to the red rectangle.

LISTING 6.3 CSS3Background2.css

```
#myCanvas {
    position: relative; top: 0px; left: 0px;

   background-color:white;
   background-image:
   radial-gradient(red 4px, transparent 18px),
   repeating-radial-gradient(red 0px,   green 4px, yellow 8px,
                               blue 12px, transparent 28px,
                               green 20px, red 24px,
                               transparent 28px,
                               transparent 32px),
   repeating-radial-gradient(red 0px,   green 4px, yellow 8px,
                               blue 12px, transparent 28px,
                               green 20px, red 24px,
                               transparent 28px,
                               transparent 32px);
   background-size: 50px 60px, 70px 80px;
   background-position: 0 0;
   box-shadow:  30px 30px 30px #000;

   resize:both;
   overflow:auto;
}

#myCanvas:hover {
    position: relative; top: 0px; left: 0px;

   background-color:white;
   background-image:
      radial-gradient(red 4px, transparent 48px),
      repeating-radial-gradient(red 2px,   green 4px, yellow 8px,
                                blue 12px, transparent 16px,
                                red 20px, blue 24px,
                                transparent 28px,
                                transparent 32px),
      radial-gradient(blue 8px, transparent 68px);

   background-size: 120px 120px, 4px 4px;
   background-position: 0 0;
}
```

Listing 6.3 contains two similar CSS3 selectors for rendering the HTML5 <canvas> element defined in Listing 6.3, also a hover-based selector that changes the background of the HTML5 <canvas> element whenever users hover over this element with their mouse. The #myCanvas selector defines a radial gradient, followed by two repeating radial gradients that specify various combinations of red, green, yellow, and blue at different pixel locations. A key point involves the use of transparent, which changes the gap between consecutive colors that are rendered.

As you can see in the definition of the #myCanvas selector, there are many possible combinations available for the colors, the gradients (and their types), and the colors for the gradients, along with the values for the background-size attribute. There is no "right" way to define these patterns; feel free to experiment with different combinations, and you might create unexpectedly pleasing results.

Figure 6.2 displays a set of randomly generated rectangles with a shadow effect based on RandRectanglesShadow.html in Listing 6.2.

FIGURE 6.2 Canvas random rectangles.

HTML5 CANVAS LINEAR GRADIENTS

HTML5 Canvas provides two primary types of color gradients (similar to SVG and CSS3): *linear gradients* and *radial gradients*.

Linear color gradients can be further sub-divided into three types: horizontal linear gradients, vertical linear gradients, and diagonal linear gradients. Thus, HTML5 Canvas provides color gradients that enable you to create pleasing visual effects.

A linear gradient is defined in terms of addColorStop elements, each of which contains a decimal (between 0 and 1) and a hexadecimal value that represents a color. For example, if you define a linear gradient with an initial color of #FF0000 (the hexadecimal value for red) and a final color of #000000 (the hexadecimal value for black), then the resultant color gradient will range (in a linear fashion) from red to black. Linear gradients enable you to create vivid and interesting color combinations, and they are available in three varieties: horizontal, vertical, and diagonal. Note that "linear gradient" and "linear color gradient" are used interchangeably in this book.

Horizontal, Vertical, and Diagonal Linear Gradients

As you learned in the introduction of this chapter, HTML5 Canvas supports the method createLinearGradient() that you can use to programmatically create linear gradients, and its syntax looks like this:

```
context.createLinearGradient(startX, startY, endX, endY);
```

The HTML5 Web page LGradRectangles1.html in Listing 6.4 demonstrates how to render a set of rectangles with horizontal, vertical, and diagonal

linear gradients. Listing 6.4 references the CSS3 stylesheet `HoverAnima-`
`tion1.css` that applies CSS3 `keyframes`-based 2D animation to the first
HTML5 `<canvas>` element whenever users hover over this `<canvas>` element with their mouse. Listing 6.4 also references the CSS3 stylesheet `Hov-`
`erAnimation2.css`, which acts in a similar fashion; however, this stylesheet
applies CSS3 3D animation effects to the second HTML5 `<canvas>` element
in Listing 6.4. Since the animation techniques in these CSS stylesheets are discussed in Chapter 2, we will omit them from this chapter, but the entire source
code is available on the companion disc.

LISTING 6.4 *LGradRectangles1.html*

```
<!DOCTYPE html>
<html lang="en">
 <head>
  <meta charset="utf-8">
  <title>Canvas Linear Gradient Rectangles</title>
  <link href="HoverAnimation1.css" rel="stylesheet"
     type="text/css">
  <link href="HoverAnimation2.css" rel="stylesheet"
     type="text/css">

  <style>
    input {
      width:350px;
      font-size:24px;
      background-color:#f00;
    }
  </style>

  <script><!--
    window.addEventListener('load', function () {
      var elem = document.getElementById('myCanvas');
      if (!elem || !elem.getContext) {
        return;
      }

      var context = elem.getContext('2d');
      if (!context) {
        return;
      }

      var elem2 = document.getElementById('myCanvas2');
      if (!elem2 || !elem2.getContext) {
        return;
      }

      var context2 = elem2.getContext('2d');
      if (!context2) {
        return;
      }

      var basePointX = 0;
      var basePointY = 0;
      var currentX   = 0;
```

```
        var currentY   = 0;
        var rectWidth  = 200;
        var rectHeight = 200;
        var clickCount = 0;
        var gradient1;

        redrawCanvas = function() {
            // clear the canvas before drawing new set of
rectangles
            //context.clearRect(0, 0, elem.width, elem.
height);
            //context2.clearRect(0, 0, elem.width, elem.
height);

            // upper left rectangle: horizontal linear
gradient
            currentX = basePointX;
            currentY = basePointY;

            gradient1 = context.createLinearGradient(
                                    currentX,
                                    currentY,
                                    currentX+rectWidth,

currentY+0*rectHeight);

            gradient1.addColorStop(0, '#f00');
            gradient1.addColorStop(1, '#00f');
            context.fillStyle = gradient1;
            context.fillRect(currentX, currentY,
                        rectWidth, rectHeight);

            // upper right rectangle: vertical linear gradient
            currentX = basePointX+rectWidth;
            currentY = basePointY;

            gradient1 = context.createLinearGradient(currentX,
                                        currentY,

currentX+0*rectWidth,

currentY+rectHeight);

            gradient1.addColorStop(0, '#ff0');
            gradient1.addColorStop(1, '#00f');
            context.fillStyle = gradient1;
            context.fillRect(currentX, currentY,
                        rectWidth, rectHeight);

            // render the lower rectangles in the second
                <canvas> element
            // lower left rectangle: diagonal linear gradient
            currentX = basePointX;
            currentY = basePointY;
        //currentY = basePointY+rectHeight;
```

```
        gradient1 = context2.createLinearGradient(
                                currentX,
                                currentY,
                                currentX+rectWidth,

 currentY+rectHeight);

        gradient1.addColorStop(0,   '#f00');
        gradient1.addColorStop(0.5,'#0f0');
        gradient1.addColorStop(1,   '#00f');
        context2.fillStyle = gradient1;
        context2.fillRect(currentX, currentY,
                          rectWidth, rectHeight);

        // lower right rectangle: diagonal linear gradient
        currentX = basePointX+rectWidth;
        currentY = basePointY;
        //currentY = basePointY+rectHeight;

        gradient1 = context2.createLinearGradient(
                                currentX+rectWidth,
                                currentY,
                                currentX+0*rectWidth,
                                currentY+rectHeight);

        gradient1.addColorStop(0,   '#fff');
        gradient1.addColorStop(0.3,'#000');
        gradient1.addColorStop(0.6,'#ff0');
        gradient1.addColorStop(1,   '#f00');
        context2.fillStyle = gradient1;
        context2.fillRect(currentX, currentY,
                          rectWidth, rectHeight);

        ++clickCount;
        basePointX += 4;
        basePointY += 2;
      }

      // render linear gradient rectangles
      redrawCanvas();
    });
    // --></script>
  </head>

<body>
   <div>
     <canvas id="myCanvas" width="600" height="250">No
support for Canvas
           alt="Rendering linear gradient rectangles.">
     </canvas>
   </div>

   <div>
     <canvas id="myCanvas2" width="600" height="250">No
support for Canvas
           alt="Rendering linear gradient rectangles.">
```

```
    </canvas>
    </div>

    <div>
      <input type="button" onclick="redrawCanvas();return
false"
            value="Redraw the Rectangles" />
    </div>
  </body>
</html>
```

Listing 6.4 renders four rectangles with linear gradient shading. The linear gradients have two, three, or four invocations of the `addColorStop()` method, using various combinations of colors (expressed in hexadecimal form) so that you can see some of the gradient effects that are possible.

Experiment with different values for the color stop definitions to see how their values change the appearance of the rendered rectangles.

Figure 6.3 displays a set of randomly generated rectangles with a shadow effect based on `LGradRectangles1.html` in Listing 6.4.

FIGURE 6.3 Linear gradient rectangles.

HTML5 CANVAS RADIAL GRADIENTS

A radial color gradient is the second type of HTML5 `Canvas`-based color gradient, and you can define a radial color gradient via the `createRadial-Gradient()` method, using the `addColorStop()` method to add color values, and its syntax (without the `addColorStop()` method) looks like this:

```
context.createRadialGradient(startCenterX, startCenterY,
                             startRadius, endsCenterX,
                             endCenterY, endRadius);
```

A *radial* color gradient can be compared to the ripple effect that is created when you drop a stone in a pond, where each "ripple" has a color that changes in a gradient fashion. Each ripple corresponds to a color stop element. For example, if you define a radial gradient with a start color of #FF0000 (which is red) and an end color of #000000 (which is black), then the resultant color gradient will range—in a radial fashion—from red to black. Radial gradients can also contain multiple start/stop color combinations. The point to keep in mind is that radial gradients change colors in a *linear* fashion, but the rendered colors are drawn in an expanding *radial* fashion. Note that "radial gradient" and "radial color gradient" are used interchangeably in this book.

Listing 6.5 displays the contents of the HTML5 page RGradRectangles1.html that renders line segments, rectangles, and circles in an HTML5 <canvas> element using linear and radial gradients.

LISTING 6.5 RGradRectangles1.html

```
<!DOCTYPE html>
<html lang="en">
 <head>
  <meta charset="utf-8">
  <title>Canvas Radial Gradient Rectangles</title>
  <link href="HoverAnimation1.css" rel="stylesheet"
                                    type="text/css">

  <style>
    input {
      width:300px;
      font-size:24px;
      background-color:#f00;
    }
  </style>

  <script><!--
    window.addEventListener('load', function () {
      var elem = document.getElementById('myCanvas');
      if (!elem || !elem.getContext) {
        return;
      }

      var context = elem.getContext('2d');
      if (!context) {
        return;
      }

      var basePointX = 10;
      var basePointY = 10;
      var currentX   = 0;
      var currentY   = 0;
      var rectWidth  = 200;
```

```
var rectHeight = 200;
var clickCount = 0;
var gradient1;

redrawCanvas = function() {
   // clear the canvas before drawing new set of rectangles
   //context.clearRect(0, 0, elem.width, elem.height);

   // upper left rectangle
   currentX = basePointX;
   currentY = basePointY;

   gradient1 = context.createRadialGradient
                              (currentX,
                               currentY,
                               0,
                               currentX+rectWidth,
                               currentY+rectHeight,
                               rectWidth);

   gradient1.addColorStop(0, '#f00');
   gradient1.addColorStop(1, '#00f');
   context.fillStyle = gradient1;
   context.fillRect(currentX, currentY,
                    rectWidth, rectHeight);

   // upper right rectangle
   currentX = basePointX+rectWidth;
   currentY = basePointY;

   gradient1 = context.createRadialGradient
                              (currentX,
                               currentY,
                               0,
                               currentX+rectWidth,
                               currentY+rectHeight,
                               rectWidth);

   gradient1.addColorStop(0, '#ff0');
   gradient1.addColorStop(1, '#00f');
   context.fillStyle = gradient1;
   context.fillRect(currentX, currentY,
                    rectWidth, rectHeight);

   // lower left rectangle
   currentX = basePointX;
   currentY = basePointY+rectHeight;

   gradient1 = context.createRadialGradient(
                               currentX,
                               currentY,
                               0,
                               currentX+rectWidth,
                               currentY+rectHeight,
                               rectWidth);
```

```
            gradient1.addColorStop(0,   '#f00');
            gradient1.addColorStop(0.5,'#0f0');

            gradient1.addColorStop(1,   '#00f');
            context.fillStyle = gradient1;
            context.fillRect(currentX, currentY,
                             rectWidth, rectHeight);

            // lower right rectangle
            currentX = basePointX+rectWidth;
            currentY = basePointY+rectHeight;

            gradient1 = context.createRadialGradient
                                          (currentX,
                                           currentY,
                                           0,
                                           currentX+rectWidth,
                                           currentY+rectHeight,
                                             rectWidth);

            gradient1.addColorStop(0,   '#fff');
            gradient1.addColorStop(0.3,'#000');
            gradient1.addColorStop(0.6,'#ff0');
            gradient1.addColorStop(1,   '#f00');
            context.fillStyle = gradient1;
            context.fillRect(currentX, currentY,
                             rectWidth, rectHeight);

            ++clickCount;
            basePointX += 2;
            basePointY += 2;
         }

      // render a set of rectangles
      redrawCanvas();
      });
      // --></script>
   </head>

   <body>
     <div>
      <canvas id="myCanvas" width="600" height="500">No support
                                              for Canvas
             alt="Rendering radial gradient rectangles.">
      </canvas>
      </div>

      <div>
      <input type="button" onclick="redrawCanvas();return false"
             value="Redraw the Rectangles" />
      </div>
   </body>
</html>
```

Listing 6.5 is similar to Listing 6.4, except for the use of a radial gradient (instead of a linear gradient) that ranges in a radial fashion from blue to red.

The method `addColorStop()` is invoked four times in order to add four "color stop values" to the radial gradient. Listing 6.5 also references `HoverAnimation1.css`; the entire source code for `HoverAnimation1.css` is available on the companion disc.

Figure 6.4 displays the result of rendering `RGradRectangles1.html`, which creates a set of rectangles with a radial gradient.

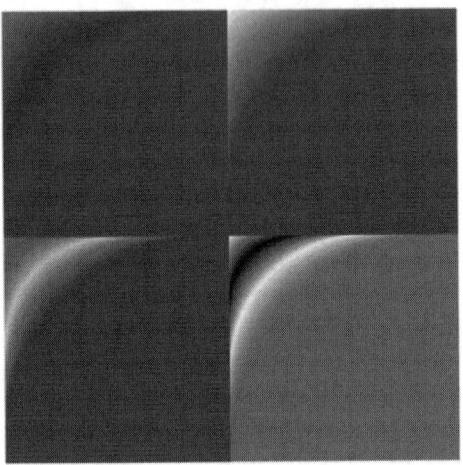

Redraw the Rectangles

FIGURE 6.4 Radial gradient rectangles.

RENDERING IMAGES ON CANVAS WITH CSS3 SELECTORS

HTML5 `Canvas` supports the rendering of binary images, and you can also apply CSS selectors to the HTML5 `<canvas>` element. Listing 6.7 displays the contents of `Image1.html`; Listing 6.8 displays the contents of `Image1.css`, whose selectors are applied to the HTML5 `<canvas>` element in Listing 6.7.

LISTING 6.7 Image1.html

```
<!DOCTYPE html>
<html lang="en">
<head>
  <meta charset="utf-8" />
  <title>Rendering Binary Images in HTML5 Canvas</title>

  <link href="Image1.css" rel="stylesheet" type="text/css">
  <link href="HoverAnimation1.css" rel="stylesheet"
                                    type="text/css">

  <script>
    function renderPNG() {
```

```
      // Get the canvas element
      var elem = document.getElementById('myCanvas');
      if (!elem || !elem.getContext) {
        return;
      }

      // Get the canvas 2d context
      var context = elem.getContext('2d');
      if (!context) {
        return;
      }

      var basePointX  = 30;
      var basePointY  = 30;
      var rectWidth   = 150;
      var rectHeight  = 200;
      var borderX     = rectWidth/2;
      var borderY     = rectHeight/2;
      var offsetX     = 20;
      var offsetY     = 20;
      var gradientR   = 60;

      // Create a radial gradient:
      var rGradient = context.createRadialGradient(
                            basePointX+rectWidth/2,
                            basePointY+rectWidth/2,
                            gradientR,
                            basePointX+rectWidth/2,
                            basePointY+rectWidth/2,
                            3*gradientR);

    rGradient.addColorStop(0,   '#FF0000');
    rGradient.addColorStop(0.5, '#FFFF00');
    rGradient.addColorStop(1,   '#000044');

      // rectangular background with radial gradient:
      context.fillStyle = rGradient;
      context.fillRect(basePointX-offsetX,
                    basePointY-offsetY,
                    rectWidth+borderX+2*offsetX,
                    rectHeight+borderY+2*offsetY);

      // Load the PNG
      var myImage = new Image();
      myImage.onload = function() {
        context.drawImage(myImage,
                      basePointX,
                      basePointY,
                      rectWidth,
                      rectHeight);
      }

      myImage.src = "sample1.png";
    }
</script>
```

```
<style type="text/css">
  canvas {
     border: 0px solid #888;
     background: #FFF;
  }
</style>
</head>

<body onload="renderPNG();">
  <header>
    <h1>Hover Over the Image</h1>
  </header>

  <div>
   <canvas id="myCanvas" width="500" height="300">No
support for Canvas
   </canvas>
   </div>
</body>
</html>
```

Listing 6.7 contains JavaScript code that creates a radial gradient rGradient with three color stops. Next, a rectangle is rendered using the radial gradient that is referenced by the variable rGradient, followed by a section of code that renders the binary image sample1.png. The inline CSS code in the <style> element renders a white background with a zero-width border (so it's invisible), but you can modify this CSS code to produce additional effects. The <body> element contains the onload attribute whose value is render-PNG(), which is a JavaScript function that renders the Binary image inside the HTML5 <canvas> element.

LISTING 6.8 Image1.css
```
#myCanvas:hover {
width:  500px;
height: 300px;
position: relative; top: 0px; left: 0px;

background-color:white;
background-image:
  radial-gradient(red 4px, transparent 24px),
  repeating-radial-gradient(red 1px,  green 4px, yellow 8px,
                            blue 12px, transparent 16px,
                            red 20px, blue 24px,
                            transparent 28px,
                            transparent 32px);
background-size: 30px 30px, 40px 40px;
background-position: 0 0;
}

#myCanvas {
width:  500px;
```

```
height: 300px;
position: relative; top: 0px; left: 0px;

background-color:white;
background-image:
  radial-gradient(black 4px, transparent 20px),
  repeating-radial-gradient(blue 1px,  yellow 4px, blue 8px,
                            red 12px, transparent 16px,
                            red 20px, blue 24px,
                            transparent 28px,
                            transparent 32px);
background-size: 30px 30px,  40px 40px;
background-position: 0 0;
}
```

The first selector in Listing 6.8 displays another pattern (based on a different radial gradient) whenever users hover with their mouse over the HTML5 `<canvas>` element. The second selector in Listing 6.8 renders a colorful pattern (also based on a radial gradient) as a background rectangle for the HTML5 `<canvas>` element.

Incidentally, HTML5 Canvas also supports a `clip()` method that enables you to "clip" binary images in various ways. Moreover, you can perform compositing effects, and you can even manipulate the individual pixels of an image file. Search the Internet for articles that describe the technical details of these effects.

Figure 6.5 displays a binary image with two radial gradient background effects.

Hover Over the Image

FIGURE 6.5 HTML5 Canvas radial PNG.

REPEATING AN IMAGE ON CANVAS WITH PATTERNS

HTML5 Canvas provides the method `createPattern(image, type)` that enables you to render a set of images according to a `pattern` type, whose values can be `repeat`, `repeat-x`, `repeat-y`, and `no-repeat`. An example of the syntax (and also how to use it) looks like this:

```
var pattern = canvas.createPattern(img,"repeat");
canvas.fillStyle = pattern;
canvas.fillRect(0,0,500,300);
```

Listing 6.8 displays the contents of `RepeatingImage1.html`, which illustrates how to repeat a binary image on an HTML5 `<canvas>` element.

LISTING 6.8 RepeatingImage1.html

```
<!DOCTYPE html>
<html lang="en">
<head>
  <meta charset="utf-8" />
  <title>Repeating Images in HTML5 Canvas</title>

  <script>
    var elem, canvas, filename = "BlueBall1.png";

    function init() {
      elem = document.getElementById("myCanvas");
      canvas = elem.getContext('2d');

      var img = new Image();
      img.src = filename;
      img.addEventListener("load", modImage, false);
    }

    function modImage(e) {
      img = e.target;
      var pattern = canvas.createPattern(img,"repeat");

      canvas.fillStyle = pattern;
      canvas.fillRect(0,0,500,300);
    }

    window.addEventListener("load", init, false);
  </script>
</head>

<body>
  <div>
   <canvas id="myCanvas" width="500" height="300">No
support for Canvas
   </canvas>
  </div>
</body>
</html>
```

Listing 6.8 contains the following line of code that invokes the JavaScript `init()` method when this Web page is loaded into a browser:
`window.addEventListener("load", init, false);`

The `init()` method finds an HTML5 `<canvas>` element in the Web page, and for simplicity, no error checking is performed (which can be handled by using code from previous examples).

The `init()` method also initializes a JavaScript variable `img` that references a binary image, and then adds an event listener that executes the JavaScript function `modImage()`, as shown here:

```
var img = new Image();
img.src = filename;
img.addEventListener("load", modImage, false);
```

Finally, the `modImage()` method invokes the `Canvas` method `createPattern()` with the parameter repeat in order to create a rectangular grid of images that is based on one PNG file (which is `BlueBall1.png` in this example), as shown here:

```
var pattern = canvas.createPattern(img,"repeat");
canvas.fillStyle = pattern;
canvas.fillRect(0,0,500,300);
```

Figure 6.6 displays `RepeatingImage1.html` in Listing 6.8 in a Chrome browser on a Macbook.

FIGURE 6.6 Repeating PNG images on a Chrome browser on a MacBook.

SUMMARY

This chapter showed you how to render line segments, rectangles, and circles in HTML5 `Canvas`. You saw how to combine HTML5 `Canvas` with CSS3 stylesheets to create animation effects. Next, you learned how to create linear and radial gradients in HTML5 `Canvas`. Finally, you learned how to embed PNG files in an HTML `Canvas` element.

CHAPTER 7

SVG ESSENTIALS

This fast-paced chapter delves into many features of SVG, which is an XML-based technology for rendering 2D shapes. Entire books have been written about SVG, and one chapter about SVG is not enough to become really proficient. As a sort of compromise, the code samples contain multiple SVG features that will save you time from having to develop them by yourself. For instance, the code sample that contains SVG transforms and gradients does not provide a detailed description of these SVG features because you have already encountered transforms and gradients in the first several chapters of this book. Consequently, you already know the concepts, and it's primarily a case of learning the SVG syntax for creating such effects. At the same time, feel free to focus on the sections that illustrate the SVG features that are of greatest interest to you.

In case you didn't already know, SVG has recently become the focus of considerable interest in Web development, in part because its feature set works well with CSS3. In addition, you can use SVG instead of PNG files (discussed in Chapter 8). SVG also provides functionality that is unavailable in CSS3, such as support for arbitrary polygons, elliptic arcs, and quadratic and cubic Bezier curves. Moreover, you can easily combine SVG with CSS3 selectors in order to create 3D graphics and animation effects.

The first part of this chapter contains code samples that illustrate how to render lines and rectangles, and also how to create linear gradients and radial gradients. The second part of this chapter discusses polygonal shapes and the highly versatile SVG `<path>` element.

The third section contains Bezier curves with SVG transforms, how to render text in SVG, and SVG filters. The final section contains examples of working with various combinations of SVG, CSS3, and jQuery, followed by a brief comparison of SVG and CSS3.

BASIC FEATURES OF SVG

SVG supports linear gradients, radial gradients, filter effects, transforms (`translate`, `scale`, `skew`, and `rotate`), Bezier curves, and animation effects. You can create SVG documents with code for rendering shapes, or you can embed SVG directly in an HTML Web page. SVG elements are inserted into the DOM of a Web page, which means that it's possible to track/manage groups of SVG elements. Some advantages of SVG include:

- No blurred/jagged edges when zooming in
- Convenient format for import/export between tools
- Can apply XSL stylesheets to SVG documents

On the other hand, keep in mind that SVG is verbose, and can be difficult to read in SVG documents that are programmatically generated. In addition, nontrivial animation effects can be cumbersome: consider using D3 for creating animation and handling mouse-related events. Although this chapter focuses on "pure" SVG, a collection of SVG code samples with JavaScript is here: *https://github.com/ocampesato/svg-graphics.*

As you will see, it's possible to match CSS selectors with SVG elements via the CSS `url()` function, and the combination of CSS3 and SVG gives you a powerful mechanism for leveraging the functionality of SVG in CSS3 selectors. In fact, you can combine CSS, SVG, D3, and HTML5 `Canvas` elements in the same HTML Web page.

RENDERING LINE SEGMENTS AND RECTANGLES IN SVG

This section shows you how to render line segments and rectangles in SVG documents. As a simple example, SVG supports a `<line>` element for rendering line segments, and its syntax looks like this:

```
<line x1="20" y1="20" x2="100" y2="150".../>
```

SVG `<line>` elements render line segments that connect the two points `(x1,y1)` and `(x2,y2)`.

SVG supports a `<rect>` element for rendering rectangles, and its syntax looks like this:

```
<rect width="200" height="50" x="20" y="50".../>
```

The SVG `<rect>` element renders a rectangle whose width and height are specified in the `width` and `height` attributes. The upper-left vertex of the rectangle is specified by the point with coordinates `(x,y)`.

Listing 7.1 displays the contents of `BasicShapes1.svg`, which illustrates how to render line segments and rectangles.

LISTING 7.1 BasicShapes1.svg

```
<?xml version="1.0" encoding="iso-8859-1"?>
<!DOCTYPE svg PUBLIC "-//W3C//DTD SVG 20001102//EN"
 "http://www.w3.org/TR/2000/CR-SVG-20001102/DTD/svg-20001102.dtd">

<svg xmlns="http://www.w3.org/2000/svg"
     xmlns:xlink="http://www.w3.org/1999/xlink"
     width="100%" height="100%">
 <g>
   <!-- left-side figures -->
   <line x1="20" y1="20" x2="220" y2="20"
         stroke="blue" stroke-width="4"/>

   <line x1="20" y1="40" x2="220" y2="40"
         stroke="red" stroke-width="10"/>

   <rect width="200" height="50" x="20" y="70"
         fill="red" stroke="black" stroke-width="4"/>

   <path d="M20,150 l200,0 l0,50 l-200,0 z"
         fill="blue" stroke="red" stroke-width="4"/>

   <!-- right-side figures -->
   <path d="M250,20 l200,0 l-100,50 z"
         fill="blue" stroke="red" stroke-width="4"/>

   <path d="M300,100 l100,0 l50,50 l-50,50 l-100,0 l-50,-50 z"
         fill="yellow" stroke="red" stroke-width="4"/>
 </g>
</svg>
```

The first SVG <line> element in Listing 7.1 specifies the color blue and a stroke-width (i.e., line width) of 4, whereas the second SVG <line> element specifies the color red and a stroke-width of 10.

Notice that the first SVG <rect> element renders a rectangle that looks the same (except for the color) as the second SVG <line> element, which shows that it's possible to use different SVG elements to render a rectangle (or a line segment).

The SVG <path> element is probably the most flexible and powerful element because you can create arbitrarily complex shapes, based on a "concatenation" of other SVG elements. Later in this chapter you will see an example of how to render multiple Bezier curves in an SVG <path> element.

An SVG <path> element contains a d attribute that specifies the points in the desired path. For example, the first SVG <path> element in Listing 7.1 contains the following d attribute:

d="M20,150 l200,0 l0,50 l-200,0 z"

This is how to interpret the contents of the d attribute:

- Move to the absolute location point (20,150)
- Draw a horizontal line segment 200 pixels to the right
- Draw a line segment by moving 10 pixels to the right and 50 pixels down

- Draw a horizontal line segment by moving 200 pixels toward the left
- Draw a line segment to the initial point (specified by z)

Similar comments apply to the other two SVG `<path>` elements in Listing 7.1. One thing to keep in mind is that uppercase letters (C, L, M, and Q) refer to absolute positions whereas lowercase letters (c, l, m, and q) refer to relative positions with respect to the element that is to the immediate left. Experiment with the code in Listing 7.1 by using combinations of lowercase and uppercase letters to gain a better understanding of how to create different visual effects.

Figure 7.1 displays the result of rendering the SVG document `Basic-Shapes1.svg`.

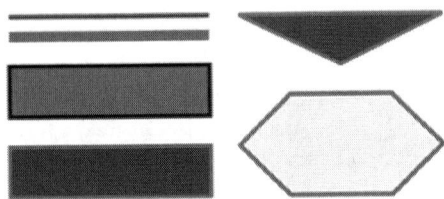

FIGURE 7.1 SVG lines and rectangles.

SVG GRADIENTS

As you have probably surmised, SVG supports linear gradients as well as radial gradients that you can apply to 2D shapes.

Listing 7.2 displays the contents of `BasicShapesLRG1.svg`, which illustrates how to render 2D shapes with linear gradients and with radial gradients.

LISTING 7.2 BasicShapesLRG1.svg

```
<?xml version="1.0" encoding="iso-8859-1"?>
<!DOCTYPE svg PUBLIC "-//W3C//DTD SVG 20001102//EN"
 "http://www.w3.org/TR/2000/CR-SVG-20001102/DTD/svg-
20001102.dtd">

<svg xmlns="http://www.w3.org/2000/svg"
     xmlns:xlink="http://www.w3.org/1999/xlink"
     width="100%" height="100%">
  <defs>
    <linearGradient id="pattern1"
                    x1="0%" y1="100%" x2="100%" y2="0%">
      <stop offset="0%"   stop-color="yellow"/>
      <stop offset="40%"  stop-color="red"/>
      <stop offset="80%"  stop-color="blue"/>
    </linearGradient>

    <radialGradient id="pattern2">
      <stop offset="0%"   stop-color="yellow"/>
      <stop offset="40%"  stop-color="red"/>
      <stop offset="80%"  stop-color="blue"/>
    </radialGradient>
  </defs>
```

```
<g>
 <ellipse cx="120" cy="80" rx="100" ry="50"
          fill="url(#pattern1)"/>

 <ellipse cx="120" cy="200" rx="100" ry="50"
          fill="url(#pattern2)"/>

 <ellipse cx="320" cy="80" rx="50" ry="50"
          fill="url(#pattern2)"/>

 <ellipse cx="450" cy="240" rx="50" ry="50"
          fill="url(#pattern1)"/>
</g>
</svg>
```

Listing 7.2 contains an SVG <defs> element that specifies a <linearGradient> element (whose id attribute has value pattern1) with three stop values using an XML-based syntax, followed by a <radialGradient> element with three <stop> elements and an id attribute whose value is pattern2.

The SVG <g> element contains four <ellipse> elements, the first of which specifies the point (120,80) as its center (cx,cy), with a major radius of 100, a minor radius of 50, filled with the linear gradient pattern1, as shown here:

```
<ellipse cx="120" cy="80" rx="100" ry="50"
         fill="url(#pattern1)"/>
```

Similar comments apply to the other three SVG <ellipse> elements.

Figure 7.2 displays the result of rendering BasicShapesLRG1.svg.

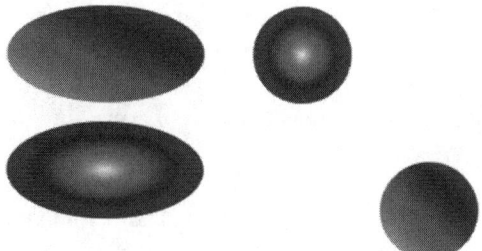

FIGURE 7.2 SVG linear radial gradient arcs.

THE SVG <PATTERN> ELEMENT

The SVG <pattern> element enables you to define custom patterns that can create surprisingly rich visual effects with relatively simple code.

Listing 7.3 displays the contents of PatternElement1.svg, which illustrates how to render a rectangle and an ellipse with different custom patterns.

LISTING 7.3 PatternElement1.svg

```
<?xml version="1.0" encoding="iso-8859-1"?>
<!DOCTYPE svg PUBLIC "-//W3C//DTD SVG 20001102//EN"
```

```
               "http://www.w3.org/TR/2000/CR-SVG-20001102/DTD/
                 svg-20001102.dtd">

<svg xmlns="http://www.w3.org/2000/svg"
       xmlns:xlink="http://www.w3.org/1999/xlink"
       width="100%" height="100%">
  <defs>
    <pattern id="dotPattern1" width="8" height="8"
              patternUnits="userSpaceOnUse">
       <circle id="circle1" cx="2" cy="2" r="3"
               style="fill:blue;"/>
    </pattern>

    <pattern id="dotPattern2" width="8" height="8"
              patternUnits="userSpaceOnUse">
     <rect x="0" y="0" width="4" height="4" fill="red" />
     <rect x="4" y="0" width="4" height="4" fill="black" />
     <rect x="0" y="4" width="4" height="4" fill="black" />
     <rect x="4" y="4" width="4" height="4" fill="red" />
    </pattern>
  </defs>

  <g id="largeCylinder" transform="translate(100,20)">
     <rect x="0" y="0" width="200" height="100"
           style="fill:url(#dotPattern1)"/>

     <ellipse cx="100" cy="150" rx="80"  ry="40"
              stroke="blue" stroke-width="4"
              style="fill:url(#dotPattern2)"/>
  </g>
</svg>
```

Listing 7.3 contains an SVG `<defs>` element that in turn contains two `<pattern>` elements. The first `<pattern>` element creates a "dotted" effect, where each "dot" is a blue circle of radius 3. The second `<pattern>` element creates a "checkerboard" pattern by specifying four rectangles of equal dimensions, whose colors are red and black in the first "row," and black and red in the second "row."

The next section in Listing 7.3 contains an SVG `<g>` element that contains a `<rect>` element whose fill attribute specifies the first `<pattern>` element, followed by an `<ellipse>` element whose fill attribute specifies the second `<pattern>` element.

Figure 7.3 displays the result of rendering the rectangle and ellipse that are defined in the SVG document `Pattern1.svg`.

FIGURE 7.3 Two shapes rendered with different patterns.

SVG <POLYGON> AND <POLYLINE> ELEMENTS

The SVG <polygon> element contains a polygon attribute in which you can specify points that represent the vertices of a polygon. The SVG <polygon> element is most useful when you want to create polygons with an arbitrary number of sides, but you can also use this element to render line segments and rectangles.

The syntax of the SVG <polygon> element looks like this:

```
<polygon path="specify a list of points" fill="..." />
```

Listing 7.4 displays the contents of a portion of SvgCube1.svg that illustrates how to render a cube in SVG.

LISTING 7.4 SvgCube1.svg

```
<?xml version="1.0" encoding="iso-8859-1"?>
<!DOCTYPE svg PUBLIC "-//W3C//DTD SVG 20001102//EN"
 "http://www.w3.org/TR/2000/CR-SVG-20001102/DTD/svg-
    20001102.dtd">

<svg xmlns="http://www.w3.org/2000/svg"
    xmlns:xlink="http://www.w3.org/1999/xlink"
    width="100%" height="100%">
  <!-- <defs> element omitted for brevity -->

  <!-- top face (counter clockwise) -->
  <polygon fill="url(#pattern1)"
          points="50,50 200,50 240,30 90,30"/>

  <!-- front face -->
  <rect width="150" height="150" x="50" y="50"
        fill="url(#pattern2)"/>

  <!-- right face (counter clockwise) -->
  <polygon fill="url(#pattern3)"
          points="200,50 200,200 240,180 240,30"/>
</svg>
```

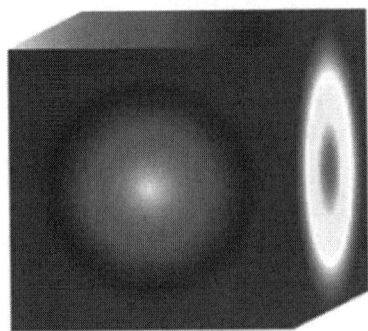

FIGURE 7.4 An SVG gradient cube.

Listing 7.4 contains an SVG `<g>` element that contains the three faces of a cube, in which an SVG `<polygon>` element renders the top face (which is a parallelogram), an SVG `<rect>` element renders the front face, and another SVG `<polygon>` element renders the right face (which is also a parallelogram). The three faces of the cube are rendered with the linear gradient and the two radial gradients defined in the SVG `<defs>` element (not shown in Listing 7.4).

Figure 7.4 displays the result of rendering the SVG document `SvgCube1.svg`.

The SVG `<polyline>` element specifies a set of points that represent the endpoints of one or more line segments that are displayed as a connected line. The syntax of the SVG `<polyline>` element is very similar to the SVG `<polygon>` element, as in the following example:

```
<polyline points="50,50 200,50 200,200, 50, 200"
          fill="url(#pattern2)"/>
```

The preceding code snippet renders the same "front face" rectangle as the `<rect>` element in Listing 7.4. The companion disc contains the SVG document `Polyline1.svg`, which renders the same cube as the code in Listing 7.4. `Polyline.svg` uses three `<polyline>` elements, whereas `SvgCube1.svg` uses two `<polygon>` elements and one `<rect>` element to render a cube.

SVG <PATH> ELEMENT

The SVG `<path>` element enables you to define elliptic arcs (using the d attribute) and then specify gradient effects. The SVG `<path>` element contains a d attribute for specifying path elements, as shown here:

```
<path d="specify a list of path elements" fill="..." />
```

Listing 7.5 displays the contents of `PathElement.svg`, which illustrates how to use the `<path>` element in order to render elliptic arcs.

LISTING 7.5 PathElement.svg
```
<?xml version="1.0" encoding="iso-8859-1"?>
<!DOCTYPE svg PUBLIC "-//W3C//DTD SVG 20001102//EN"
```

```
  "http://www.w3.org/TR/2000/CR-SVG-20001102/DTD/
    svg-20001102.dtd">

<svg xmlns="http://www.w3.org/2000/svg"
    xmlns:xlink="http://www.w3.org/1999/xlink"
    width="100%" height="100%">
  <defs>
    <linearGradient id="pattern1"
                    x1="0%" y1="100%" x2="100%" y2="0%">
      <stop offset="0%"   stop-color="yellow"/>
      <stop offset="40%"  stop-color="red"/>
      <stop offset="80%"  stop-color="blue"/>
    </linearGradient>
  </defs>

  <g>
   <path d="M 505,145 v -100 a 250,100 0 0,1 -200,100"
         fill="black"/>

   <path d="M 500,140 v -100 a 250,100 0 0,1 -200,100"
         fill="url(#pattern1)"
         stroke="black" stroke-thickness="8"/>

   <path d="M 305,165 v  100 a 250,100 0 0,1  200,-100"
         fill="black"/>

   <path d="M 300,160 v  100 a 250,100 0 0,1  200,-100"
         fill="url(#pattern1)"
         stroke="black" stroke-thickness="8"/>
  </g>
</svg>
```

Listing 7.5 contains an SVG `<defs>` element that defines a linear gradient, followed by an SVG `<g>` element that contains four `<path>` elements. Each `<path>` element displays an elliptic arc and references the linear gradient for the value of the fill attribute.

The first `<path>` element specifies a black background for the elliptic arc defined with the following d attribute:

```
d="M 505,145 v -100 a 250,100 0 0,1 -200,100"
```

Unfortunately, the SVG syntax for elliptic arcs is non-intuitive, and it's based on the notion of major arcs and minor arcs that connect two points on an ellipse. This example is only for illustrative purposes, so we won't delve into a detailed explanation of how elliptic arcs are defined in SVG. If you need to learn the details, you can perform an Internet search and read the information in the various links (and be prepared to spend some time experimenting with your own code samples).

The second SVG `<path>` element renders the same elliptic arc with a slight offset, using the linear gradient pattern1, which creates a shadow effect.

Similar comments apply to the other pair of SVG `<path>` elements, which render an elliptic arc with the radial gradient pattern2 (also with a shadow effect).

Figure 7.5 displays the result of rendering the SVG document `PathElement.svg`.

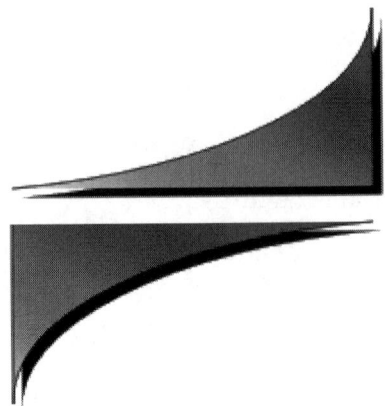

FIGURE 7.5 SVG elliptic arcs.

BEZIER CURVES AND TRANSFORMS

SVG supports quadratic and cubic Bezier curves that you can render with linear gradients or radial gradients. You can also concatenate multiple Bezier curves using an SVG `<path>` element. Listing 7.6 displays the contents of `BezierCurves1.svg`, which illustrates how to render various Bezier curves. Note that the transform-related effects are discussed later in this chapter.

LISTING 7.6 BezierCurves1.svg
```
<?xml version="1.0" encoding="iso-8859-1"?>
<!DOCTYPE svg PUBLIC "-//W3C//DTD SVG 20001102//EN"
 "http://www.w3.org/TR/2000/CR-SVG-20001102/DTD/svg-
20001102.dtd">

<svg xmlns="http://www.w3.org/2000/svg"
    xmlns:xlink="http://www.w3.org/1999/xlink"
    width="100%" height="100%">
 <!-- <defs> element omitted for brevity -->

 <g transform="scale(1.5,0.5)">
  <path d="m 0,50 C 400,200 200,-150 100,350"
        stroke="black" stroke-width="4"
        fill="url(#pattern1)"/>
 </g>

 <g transform="translate(50,50)">
   <g transform="scale(0.5,1)">
    <path d="m 50,50 C 400,100 200,200 100,20"
         fill="red" stroke="black" stroke-width="4"/>
   </g>

   <g transform="scale(1,1)">
    <path d="m 50,50 C 400,100 200,200 100,20"
         fill="yellow" stroke="black" stroke-width="4"/>
   </g>
```

```
    </g>

    <g transform="translate(-50,50)">
      <g transform="scale(1,2)">
       <path d="M 50,50 C 400,100 200,200 100,20"
             fill="blue" stroke="black" stroke-width="4"/>
      </g>
    </g>

    <g transform="translate(-50,50)">
     <g transform="scale(0.5, 0.5) translate(195,345)">
      <path d="m20,20 C20,50 20,450 300,200 s-150,-250 200,100"
            fill="blue" style="stroke:#880088;stroke-
                                width:4;"/>
     </g>

     <g transform="scale(0.5, 0.5) translate(185,335)">
      <path d="m20,20 C20,50 20,450 300,200 s-150,-250 200,100"
            fill="url(#pattern2)"
            style="stroke:#880088;stroke-width:4;"/>
     </g>

     <g transform="scale(0.5, 0.5) translate(180,330)">
      <path d="m20,20 C20,50 20,450 300,200 s-150,-250 200,100"
        fill="blue" style="stroke:#880088;stroke-width:4;"/>
     </g>

     <g transform="scale(0.5, 0.5) translate(170,320)">
      <path d="m20,20 C20,50 20,450 300,200 s-150,-250 200,100"
            fill="url(#pattern2)" style="stroke:black;
                                stroke-width:4;"/>
     </g>
    </g>

    <g transform="scale(0.8,1) translate(380,120)">
     <path d="M0,0 C200,150 400,300 20,250"
           fill="url(#pattern2)" style="stroke:blue;
                                stroke-width:4;"/>
    </g>

    <g transform="scale(2.0,2.5) translate(150,-80)">
     <path d="M200,150 C0,0 400,300 20,250"
           fill="url(#pattern2)" style="stroke:blue;
                                stroke-width:4;"/>
    </g>
</svg>
```

Listing 7.6 contains an SVG <defs> element that defines two linear gradients, followed by ten SVG <path> elements, each of which renders a cubic Bezier curve. The SVG <path> elements are enclosed in SVG <g> elements whose transform attribute contains the SVG scale() function or the SVG translate() function (or both).

The first SVG <g> element invokes the SVG scale() function to scale the cubic Bezier curve that is specified in an SVG <path> element, as shown here:

```
<g transform="scale(1.5,0.5)">
  <path d="m 0,50 C 400,200 200,-150 100,350"
        stroke="black" stroke-width="4"
        fill="url(#pattern1)"/>
</g>
```

The preceding cubic Bezier curve has an initial point (0,50), with control points (400,200) and (200,-150), followed by the second control point (100,350). The Bezier curve is black, with a width of 4, and its fill attribute is the color defined in the <linearGradient> element (whose id attribute is pattern1) that is defined in the SVG <defs> element.

The remaining SVG <path> elements are similar to the first SVG <path> element, so they will not be described.

Figure 7.6 displays the result of rendering the Bezier curves that are defined in the SVG document BezierCurves1.svg.

FIGURE 7.6 SVG Bezier curves.

RENDERING TEXT ON A PATH IN SVG

You can create nice filter effects that you can apply to 2D shapes as well as text strings.

Listing 7.7 displays the contents of the document TextOnQBezierPath1.svg, which illustrates how to render a text string along the path of a quadratic Bezier curve.

LISTING 7.7 TextOnQBezierPath1.svg

```
<?xml version="1.0" encoding="iso-8859-1"?>
<!DOCTYPE svg PUBLIC "-//W3C//DTD SVG 20001102//EN"
 "http://www.w3.org/TR/2000/CR-SVG-20001102/DTD/svg-20001102.dtd">

<svg xmlns="http://www.w3.org/2000/svg"
     xmlns:xlink="http://www.w3.org/1999/xlink"
     width="100%" height="100%">
<defs>
  <path id="pathDefinition" d="m0,0 Q100,0 200,200 T300,200 z"/>
</defs>

<g transform="translate(100,100)">
  <text id="textStyle" fill="red"
      stroke="blue" stroke-width="2"
      font-size="24">
```

```
<textPath xlink:href="#pathDefinition">
Sample Text that follows a path specified by a Quadratic
  Bezier curve
</textPath>
  </text>
</g>
</svg>
```

The SVG `<defs>` element in Listing 7.7 contains an SVG `<path>` element that defines a quadratic Bezier curve (note the `Q` in the `d` attribute). This SVG `<path>` element has an `id` attribute whose value is `pathDefinition`, which is referenced later in this code sample.

The SVG `<g>` element contains an SVG `<text>` element that specifies a text string to render, as well as an SVG `<textPath>` element that specifies the path along which the text is rendered, as shown here:

```
<textPath xlink:href="#pathDefinition">
  Sample Text that follows a path specified by a Quadratic
Bezier curve
</textPath>
```

Notice that the SVG `<textPath>` element contains the attribute `xlink:href` whose value is `pathDefinition`, which is also the `id` of the SVG `<path>` element that is defined in the SVG `<defs>` element. As a result, the text string is rendered along the path of a quadratic Bezier curve instead of rendering the text string horizontally (which is the default behavior).

Figure 7.7 displays the result of rendering `TextOnQBezierPath1.svg`, which renders a text string along the path of a quadratic Bezier curve.

FIGURE 7.7 SVG text on a quadratic Bezier.

SVG FILTERS

SVG supports a rich set of filter effects whose complete explanation can easily span more than a chapter. A mastery of SVG filters involves a learning curve because only a few SVG filters are simple. Many filters are very sophisticated, requiring multiple non-intuitive input values. In fact, it's possible to "chain" some SVG filters: the output of one filter can be the input of another filter (and the input for some SVG filters requires the output from two filters). As you might surmise, some SVG filters can be computationally intense, which in turn can adversely affect performance; in the case of mobile devices, applications that contain such filters can adversely affect battery life as well.

The list of filter-related SVG elements includes: feBlend, feColor-Matrix, feComponentTransfer, feComposite, feConvolveMatrix, feDiffuseLighting, feDisplacementMap, feFlood, feGaussianBlur, feImage, feMerge, feMorphology, feOffset, feSpecularLighting, feTile, and feTurbulence.

You can render 2D shapes as well as text strings with filter effects. Listing 7.8 displays the contents of the SVG document BlurFilterText1.svg, which renders a text string with a Blur filter.

LISTING 7.8 BlurFilterText1.svg

```
<?xml version="1.0" encoding="iso-8859-1"?>
<!DOCTYPE svg PUBLIC "-//W3C//DTD SVG 20001102//EN"
 "http://www.w3.org/TR/2000/CR-SVG-20001102/DTD/svg-
20001102.dtd">

<svg xmlns="http://www.w3.org/2000/svg"
     xmlns:xlink="http://www.w3.org/1999/xlink"
     width="100%" height="100%">
  <defs>
  <filter
      id="blurFilter1"
      filterUnits="objectBoundingBox"
      x="0" y="0"
      width="100%" height="100%">
      <feGaussianBlur stdDeviation="4"/>
  </filter>
  </defs>

<g transform="translate(50,100)">
  <text id="normalText" x="0" y="0"
      fill="red" stroke="black" stroke-width="4"
      font-size="72">
    Normal Text
  </text>

  <text id="horizontalText" x="0" y="100"
      filter="url(#blurFilter1)"
      fill="red" stroke="black" stroke-width="4"
      font-size="72">
    Blurred Text
  </text>
</g>
</svg>
```

The SVG <defs> element in Listing 7.8 contains an SVG <filter> element that specifies a Gaussian blur with the following line:

```
<feGaussianBlur stdDeviation="4"/>
```

You can specify larger values for the `stdDeviation` attribute if you want to create more "diffuse" filter effects.

The first SVG `<text>` element that is contained in the SVG `<g>` element renders a normal text string, whereas the second SVG `<text>` element contains a `filter` attribute that references the filter (defined in the SVG `<defs>` element) in order to render the same text string, as shown here:

```
filter="url(#blurFilter1)"
```

Figure 7.8 displays the result of rendering `BlurFilterText1.svg`, which creates a filter effect.

Normal Text

Blurred Text

FIGURE 7.8 SVG filter effect.

A GitHub repository with fun examples of SVG filters is here: *https://github. com/ocampesato/svg-filters-graphics*.

An extensive article that discusses various SVG filters is here: *http://www. smashingmagazine.com/2015/05/why-the-svg-filter-is-awesome/*.

A tabular list of support for SVG filters in modern browsers is here: *http:// caniuse.com/#feat=svg-filters*.

SVG TRANSFORMS AND GRADIENTS

Earlier in this chapter you saw some examples of SVG transform effects. In addition to the SVG functions `scale()`, `translate()`, and `rotate()`, SVG provides the `skew()` function to create skew effects.

Listing 7.9 displays the contents of `TransformEffects1.svg`, which illustrates how to apply transforms to rectangles and circles in SVG.

LISTING 7.9 TransformEffects1.svg

```
<?xml version="1.0" encoding="iso-8859-1"?>
<!DOCTYPE svg PUBLIC "-//W3C//DTD SVG 20001102//EN"
 "http://www.w3.org/TR/2000/CR-SVG-20001102/DTD/svg-
20001102.dtd">

<svg xmlns="http://www.w3.org/2000/svg"
     xmlns:xlink="http://www.w3.org/1999/xlink"
     width="100%" height="100%">
<defs>
  <linearGradient id="gradientDefinition1"
     x1="0" y1="0" x2="200" y2="0"
     gradientUnits="userSpaceOnUse">
     <stop offset="0%"   style="stop-color:#FF0000"/>
     <stop offset="100%" style="stop-color:#440000"/>
  </linearGradient>
```

```
      <pattern id="dotPattern" width="8" height="8"
             patternUnits="userSpaceOnUse">

         <circle id="circle1" cx="2" cy="2" r="2"
            style="fill:red;"/>
      </pattern>
   </defs>

<!-- full cylinder -->
<g id="largeCylinder" transform="translate(100,20)">
   <ellipse cx="0"   cy="50" rx="20" ry="50"
            stroke="blue" stroke-width="4"
            style="fill:url(#gradientDefinition1)"/>

   <rect x="0" y="0" width="300" height="100"
          style="fill:url(#gradientDefinition1)"/>

   <rect x="0" y="0" width="300" height="100"
          style="fill:url(#dotPattern)"/>

   <ellipse cx="300" cy="50" rx="20"  ry="50"
            stroke="blue" stroke-width="4"
            style="fill:yellow;"/>
</g>

<!-- half-sized cylinder -->
<g transform="translate(100,100) scale(.5)">
   <use xlink:href="#largeCylinder" x="0" y="0"/>
</g>

<!-- skewed cylinder -->
<g transform="translate(100,100) skewX(40) skewY(20)">
   <use xlink:href="#largeCylinder" x="0" y="0"/>
</g>

<!-- rotated cylinder -->
<g transform="translate(100,100) rotate(40)">
   <use xlink:href="#largeCylinder" x="0" y="0"/>
</g>
</svg>
```

The SVG `<defs>` element in Listing 7.9 contains a `<linearGradient>` element that defines a linear gradient, followed by an SVG `<pattern>` element that defines a custom pattern, which is shown here:

```
<pattern id="dotPattern" width="8" height="8"
      patternUnits="userSpaceOnUse">

   <circle id="circle1" cx="2" cy="2" r="2"
         style="fill:red;"/>
</pattern>
```

As you can see, the SVG `<pattern>` element contains an SVG `<circle>` element that is repeated in a grid-like fashion inside an 8x8 rectangle (note the values of the width attribute and the height attribute). The SVG `<pattern>`

element has an id attribute whose value is dotPattern because (as you will see) this element creates a "dotted" effect.

Listing 7.9 contains four SVG <g> elements, each of which renders a cylinder that references the SVG <pattern> element that is defined in the SVG <defs> element.

The first SVG <g> element in Listing 7.9 contains two SVG <ellipse> elements and two SVG <rect> elements. The first <ellipse> element renders the left-side "cover" of the cylinder with the linear gradient that is defined in the SVG <defs> element. The first <rect> element renders the "body" of the cylinder with a linear gradient, and the second <rect> element renders the "dot pattern" on the body of the cylinder. Finally, the second <ellipse> element renders the right-side "cover" of the ellipse.

The other three cylinders are easy to create: they simply reference the first cylinder and apply a transformation to change the size, shape, and orientation. Specifically, these three cylinders reference the first cylinder with the following code:

```
<use xlink:href="#largeCylinder" x="0" y="0"/>
```

and then they apply scale, skew, and rotate functions in order to render scaled, skewed, and rotated cylinders.

Figure 7.9 displays the result of rendering TransformEffects1.svg.

FIGURE 7.9 SVG Transform effects.

OTHER SVG FEATURES

SVG supports many other features, and this section describes some of them. Note that the referenced files are located on the companion disc that accompanies this book.

SVG Animation Effects

SVG supports animation effects that you can specify as part of the declaration of SVG elements. The SVG document AnimateMultiRect1.svg illustrates how to create an animation effect with four rectangles.

```
<rect id="rect1" width="100" height="100"
      stroke-width="1" stroke="blue"/>
```

```
<use xlink:href="#rect1" x="0" y="0" fill="red">
    <animate attributeName="x" attributeType="XML"
             begin="0s" dur="4s"
             fill="freeze" from="0" to="400"/>
</use>
```

The SVG `<g>` element contains an SVG `<use>` element that performs a parallel animation effect on a rectangle. The first `<use>` element references the rectangle defined in the SVG `<defs>` element and then animates the x attribute during a four-second interval. Notice that the x attribute varies from 0 to 400, which moves the rectangle horizontally from left to right. You can also animate other SVG elements, including text strings.

If you are interested in seeing how to handle zoom and pan functionality in SVG, code samples are available here: *http://msdn.microsoft.com/en-us/library/gg589508(v=vs.85).aspx.*

SVG and JavaScript

In addition to embedding "pure" SVG code in an HTML5 page, SVG allows you to embed JavaScript in a CDATA section to dynamically create SVG elements and append them to the DOM of the HTML Web page. You can also define event listeners in JavaScript for SVG elements. The SVG document `ArchEllipses1.svg` renders a set of ellipses that follow the path of an Archimedean spiral. A fragment is shown here:

```
var svgNS = "http://www.w3.org/2000/svg";

function drawSpiral(event) {
    for(angle=0; angle<maxAngle; angle+=angleDelta) {
        ellipseNode = svgDocument.createElementNS(svgNS,
                                                  "ellipse");
        ellipseNode.setAttribute("fill", redColor);
        ellipseNode.setAttribute("stroke-width",
                                            strokeWidth);
        ellipseNode.setAttribute("stroke", "yellow");

        ellipseNode.setAttribute("cx", currentX);
        ellipseNode.setAttribute("cy", currentY);
        ellipseNode.setAttribute("rx", majorAxis);
        ellipseNode.setAttribute("ry", minorAxis);
        gcNode.appendChild(ellipseNode);
    }
}
```

The SVG document `ArchEllipses1.svg` contains a CDATA section with a `<script>` element, which in turn contains the `drawSpiral()` function whose main loop renders a set of dynamically created SVG `<ellipse>` elements. Each SVG `<ellipse>` element is created in the SVG namespace that is specified in the variable `svgNS`, after which values are assigned to the required attributes of an ellipse. After each SVG `<ellipse>` element is dynamically created, the element is appended to the DOM.

Creating 3D Effects in SVG with CSS3 and JavaScript

As you learned earlier in this chapter, SVG does not support 3D effects. However, you can reference SVG elements in CSS selectors via the CSS `url()` function, which provides a powerful mechanism for leveraging the functionality of SVG in CSS3 selectors. Another technique involves a combination of JavaScript and SVG. A set of SVG code samples with 3D effects is here: *https://github.com/ocampesato/svg-filters-graphics*.

Figure 7.10 displays the result of rendering `TroughPattern3S2.svg` (which is part of the preceding open source project) in a Chrome browser on a MacBook.

FIGURE 7.10 SVG 3D "trough" shape in a Chrome browser.

If you are interested in creating 3D effects with SVG, you can get more information (including details about matrix manipulation) and code samples here: *http://msdn.microsoft.com/en-us/library/hh535759(v=vs.85).aspx*.

The open source (and very powerful) toolkit D3 is based on SVG, and many D3-based code samples are here: *https://github.com/ocampesato/d3-graphics*.

SVG, CSS, AND JQUERY

You can combine these technologies (and also with D3) in the same Web page. However, you need to add some extra code (shown later) when you dynamically create SVG elements in a Web page with jQuery. If you do not plan to use jQuery, feel free to skip this section. If you are interested in jQuery and have not worked with jQuery, read the relevant Appendix on the companion disc.

As you know by now, CSS3 selectors can reference SVG documents using the CSS3 `url()` function, which means that you can incorporate SVG-based graphics effects (including animation) in your HTML pages. The HTML Web page `Blue3DCircle1.html` references the CSS stylesheet `Blue3DCircle1.css` in order to render an SVG circle with styling effects.

As another example, the HTML5 page `CSS3SVGBarChart1.html` references the CSS3 stylesheet `CSS3SVGBarChart1.css` and the SVG document `CSS3SVGBarChart1.svg` in order to render an SVG circle, a bar chart, and multicolumn text.

An interesting scenario involves the combination of jQuery with SVG and CSS in the same Web page, as shown in the following subsections.

SVG and jQuery

Listing 7.10 displays the contents of `JQuerySVGCSSCube1.html`, which illustrates how to update the fill color of an SVG-based cube whenever users click on any of its faces.

LISTING 7.10 JQuerySVGCSSCube1.html

```html
<!DOCTYPE html>
<html lang="en">
 <head>
  <meta charset="utf-8" />
  <title>SVG, CSS, and jQuery Example</title>

  <script src="https://cdnjs.cloudflare.com/ajax/libs/
                     jquery/3.0.0-alpha1/jquery.js">
  </script>

  <style>
   .newcolor {
     fill: #c8f;
     stroke: white;
     stroke-width: 2;
   }
  </style>
 </head>

 <body>
  <svg class="none" width="600" height="300">
   <!-- top/front/right faces -->
   <polygon fill="yellow"
            points="50,50 200,50 240,30 90,30"/>
   <rect width="150" height="150" x="50" y="50"
         fill="red"/>
   <polygon fill="blue"
            points="200,50 200,200 240,180 240,30"/>
  </svg>

  <script>
    var mysvg = $("svg > *");

    $(document).ready(function() {
       mysvg.on("click", function() {
         mysvg.removeClass("none");
         $(this).toggleClass("newcolor");
         //$(this).newClass("newcolor");
       });
    });
  </script>
 </body>
</html>
```

Listing 7.10 contains boilerplate code and familiar SVG code for rendering a cube. The new code is the jQuery code block in the `<script>` element, which shows you how to define an event handler that responds to click events on any of the faces of the cube. If this code is unfamiliar to you, please read the jQuery Appendix on the companion disc.

Creating SVG Elements and jQuery

The method `document.createElement()` to add SVG DOM Nodes does not work because a namespace is required. Use the `document.createElementNS()` method, which jQuery does not handle for you.

Listing 7.11 displays the contents of `JQuerySVG.html`, which illustrates how to create an SVG ellipse and then append that ellipse to the DOM via jQuery.

LISTING 7.11 JQuerySVG.html

```
<!DOCTYPE html>
<html lang="en">
  <head>
   <meta charset="utf-8" />
   <title>An SVG Ellipse and jQuery</title>

   <script src="http://code.jquery.com/jquery-1.7.1.min.js">
   </script>
  </head>

  <body>
    <svg id="outersvg" width="800" height="500">
    </svg>

    <script>
      function createSVGElemWithNS(elem)
      {
         return document.createElementNS('http://www.
                          w3.org/2000/svg', elem);
      }

      $(document).ready(function() {
         var $mySVG = $('#outersvg');

         $(createSVGElemWithNS('circle'))
                          .attr('cx', 150)
                          .attr('cy', 100)
                          .attr('r', 50)
                          .attr('fill', 'none')
                          .attr('stroke', 'red')
                          .attr('stroke-width', 3)
                          .appendTo($mySVG);

      })
    </script>
  </body>
</html>
```

Listing 7.11 starts with boilerplate code and a `<body>` element that contains an `<svg>` element that is the container for SVG elements. The next part of the `<body>` element is a `<script>` element that starts with the JavaScript function `createSVGElemWithNS` whose sole purpose is to create elements with the SVG namespace. The second part of the `<script>` element contains the standard jQuery "ready" code block that is executed after the Web page is loaded

ON THE CD

into memory. As you can see, this code block first obtains a reference to the `<svg>` element in the Web page and then invokes the JavaScript function createSVGElemWithNS to create an SVG `<circle>` element. Method chaining is used to assign values to the SVG `<circle>` element before appending the element to the DOM.

If you want to see examples of jQuery and CSS in the same Web page, you can find such examples in the Appendix on the companion disc.

Existing SVG Elements and jQuery

The previous section showed you how to dynamically create new SVG elements and append them to the DOM with jQuery. You can also manipulate existing SVG elements with jQuery, and you can do so without having to deal with namespaces.

Listing 7.12 displays the contents of UpdateSVGViaJQuery.svg, which illustrates how to use jQuery in order to update the width attribute of an SVG `<rect>` element.

LISTING 7.12 UpdateSVGViaJQuery.svg

```
<?xml version="1.0" encoding="UTF-8" standalone="no"?>
<!DOCTYPE svg PUBLIC "-//W3C//DTD SVG 1.0//EN"
"http://www.w3.org/TR/2001/REC-SVG-20010904/DTD/svg10.dtd">

<svg xmlns="http://www.w3.org/2000/svg"
     xmlns:xlink="http://www.w3.org/1999/xlink" width="500"
                                                height="500">
   <script xlink:href="http://code.jquery.com/
                                   jquery-2.0.0b1.js">
   </script>

   <script xlink:href="http://code.jquery.com/jquery-
                                   migrate-1.1.0.js">
   </script>

   <rect id="rect1" x="50" y="50" width="200"  height="50"
    style="fill:red"/>

   <script>
      $('#rect1').attr('width', 400);
   </script>
</svg>
```

Listing 7.12 contains boilerplate code with two `<script>` elements that reference jQuery-related scripts. The `<body>` element in Listing 7.12 contains an SVG `<svg>` element that in turn contains two `<rect>` elements, followed by a `<script>` element that contains a jQuery code block. After the Web page is loaded into memory, this code block executes and sets the width attribute of the first SVG `<rect>` element to 400. This simple code sample shows you how easy it is to update attributes of SVG elements via jQuery.

jQuery Plugins for SVG

If you prefer to use jQuery instead of D3 in your HTML5 Web pages, you can add SVG support by means of jQuery plugins.

For example, the following jQuery plugin provides some SVG support: *http://keith-wood.name/svg.html*.

The following code block illustrates how to render several 2D shapes using this jQuery plugin:

```
svg.rect(50, 50, 100, 100,
         {fill: 'blue', stroke: 'red', 'stroke-width': 3});
svg.line(50, 50, 100, 100,
         {'stroke': 3, 'stroke-width': 3});
svg.circle(50, 50, 100, 100,
         {'fill': 'red', 'stroke': 3, 'stroke-width': 3});
svg.ellipse(250, 250, 100, 50,
         {'fill': 'red', 'stroke': 3, 'stroke-width': 3});
```

In the preceding code block, the JavaScript variable svg is a reference to an HTML <div> element that is defined elsewhere in an HTML5 Web page.

A jQuery plugin for animating SVG <path> elements can be found at the following sites: *http://www.jqueryrain.com/2015/10/jquery-drawsvg-animate-svg-paths/* and *http://www.justinmccandless.com/blog/Patching+jQuery's+Lack+of+SVG+Support*.

A BRIEF COMPARISON OF SVG AND CSS3

This section briefly summarizes the features that are common to SVG and CSS3 and also the features that are unique to each technology. Chapters 6 and 7 contain code samples that illustrate some of the features that are summarized in this section.

SVG and CSS3 both provide support for the following:

• Linear and radial gradients
• 2D graphics and animation effects
• The ability to create shapes such as rectangles, circles, and ellipses
• WAI-ARIA

SVG provides support for the following features that are not available in CSS3:

• Bezier curves
• Hierarchical object definitions
• Custom glyphs
• Rendering text along an arbitrary path
• Defining event listeners on SVG objects
• Programmatic creation of 2D shapes using JavaScript
• "Accessibility" to XML-based technologies and tools

CSS3 provides support for the following features that are not available in SVG:

- 3D graphics and animation effects
- Multicolumn rendering of text
- WebGL-oriented functionality (e.g., CSS Shaders)

Note that SVG Filters and CSS Filters will become one and the same at some point in the not-too-distant future.

In general, SVG is better suited than CSS3 for large data sets that will be used for data visualization, and you can reference the SVG document (which might render some type of chart) in a CSS3 selector using the CSS3 `url()` function. You have already seen such an example in Chapter 3, where the SVG document contains the layout for a bar chart. In general, there might be additional processing involved where data is retrieved or aggregated from one or more sources (such as databases and Web services), and then manipulated using some programming language (such as XSLT, Java, or JavaScript) in order to programmatically create an SVG document or perhaps create SVG elements programmatically in a browser session.

SUMMARY

This chapter started with an introduction to SVG and how to render 2D shapes using SVG. You learned about SVG gradients (linear and radial), and how to specify gradients when rendering 2D shapes. Next you learned about the SVG `<polygon>` element for rendering an arbitrary polygon (convex or concave) in the plane. You also learned about the SVG `<pattern>` element and how to create custom patterns for creating rich visual effects. Then you learned about Bezier curves and how to render text strings along a path (such as a Bezier curve) in SVG. Finally, you learned about SVG filters and how to combine them with SVG transforms and apply them to 2D shapes.

CHAPTER 8

MISCELLANEOUS TOPICS

This chapter contains an eclectic mix of topics, starting with an overview of Houdini, which is an initiative that has far-reaching implications for CSS in Web pages. You will also learn about Flexbox and Grid Layout, and performance techniques for binary images. In addition, you will see a comparison of CSS3, SVG, and HTML5 `Canvas`, as well as Web Animation APIs, and animation-related toolkits.

The first part of this chapter is a quick introduction to Houdini, which is an important task force whose goal is to provide new APIs that will provide consistent CSS behavior in all modern browsers.

The second part of this chapter contains code samples that show you how to use `CSS Flexbox` and `CSS Grid Layout`. The third part of this chapter discusses performance improvements for HTML5 Web pages and CSS3, as well as a comparison of CSS3, SVG, and HTML5 `Canvas`.

The fourth part of this chapter covers performance techniques for optimizing binary images, as well as a description of spritesheets, the blur-up technique, progressive images, and Web fonts. The fifth part of this chapter looks into the Web Animations API and other animation toolkits, such as GSAP, mojo.io, and sequence.js.

The final part of this chapter delves into some of the features of Chrome Inspector, which provides a very rich set of diagnostics and debugging capabilities. You will learn about "computed properties," how to make live updates to properties in CSS selectors, and also how to gather data that can help you pinpoint performance bottlenecks. After completing this section, you will be in a better position to make a feature-based comparison of Chrome Inspector with the corresponding features that are supported in other modern browsers.

PROJECT HOUDINI

Houdini is a W3C task force whose goal is to provide a set of APIs to make CSS consistent in all modern browsers. These APIs will also enable developers to extend CSS by accessing the styling and layout process of a browser's rendering engine. Although Houdini is a relatively new group, some Houdini samples are here: *https://github.com/GoogleChrome/houdini-samples*.

As you probably know by now, polyfills (such as Modernizr) are JavaScript toolkits that "fill in" missing features in browsers so that other JavaScript toolkits will operate consistently in different modern browsers. In essence, polyfills work by modifying the DOM.

The CSS "counterpart" to the DOM is the CSSOM, which is an acronym for the CSS Object Model. Unfortunately, the CSSOM is inconsistent across browsers and lacks critical features. Moreover, "polyfilling" CSS is more difficult than polyfilling the DOM (and it's also an incomplete solution).

One deficiency of the CSSOM is that it will discard any CSS rules or declarations that are not recognized; therefore, it's necessary to use the DOM (specifically to access <style> and <link> elements) in order to polyfill those rules and declarations.

In essence, the goal of Houdini is to modify the browser's internal rendering engine in order to "normalize" (i.e., eliminate inconsistent behavior of) CSS in modern browsers.

The Rendering Pipeline

The Rendering Pipeline involves the following sequence of phases (in this order):

1. Parser
2. DOM/CSSOM
3. Cascade
4. Layout
5. Paint
6. Composite

The first three phases are the components of the CSS Properties and Values API, and the last three phases comprise the Worklets. Houdini has introduced Phase 1 (not written yet) and Phase 3 in the Rendering Pipeline. Phase 1 is where external stylesheets will be handled correctly, and also where CSS custom extensions will be supported.

Houdini also introduces the notion of worklets, which are essentially scripts for handling registration-related operations. Worklets support various features, such as the ability to invoke JavaScript code.

Navigate to the Houdini home page for more detailed information about the proposed Houdini APIs.

CSS3 ADVANCED FEATURES

The CSS3 examples in this book have been tested in `WebKit`-based browsers, and you use browser-specific prefixes (which were discussed briefly in Chapter 1) to insert the CSS3 code for other browsers. In addition, some of the code samples in this chapter are rendered in Google Canary, and sometimes in a nightly build of WebKit, which will be noted accordingly. When this book goes to print, it's possible that this functionality will be available in the general Chrome distribution.

There are several CSS features that have been under active development, and most (possibly all) of them are available in `WebKit`-based browsers. In many cases, the W3C specification for each of the new CSS features is a "work in progress," so it's possible that they will be modified by the time you read this book. Check a website such as `www.caniuse.com` for information about the latest feature support in your browser of choice.

Among the advanced (and in some cases experimental) features are:

1. CSS Flexbox
2. CSS Blending
3. CSS Compositing
4. CSS Exclusions
5. CSS Regions

With the preceding points in mind, a list of some of the latest CSS3 features is here:

- CSS Canvas backgrounds (Webkit and FF)
- CSS device adaptation (IE10)
- CSS Exclusions (IE10)
- CSS Filters (IE10 and Webkit)
- CSS Flexbox (IE10)
- CSS Grid (IE10 and Webkit)
- CSS Regions (IE10 and Webkit)
- CSS Custom Filters (Webkit)
- CSS Templates (IE10)

CSS Flexbox is the only feature in the preceding list that is covered in this chapter. You will also see some CSS Flexbox code samples and screenshots that illustrate how to create graphics effects. You can find the status for the other CSS features by navigating to their respective home pages.

CSS FLEXBOX (FLEXIBLE BOX)

CSS supports several layout models, such as block, inline, table, and positioned layout models. In addition, CSS supports the CSS Flexbox (Flexible Box) model, and you will see some examples in this section.

Flexbox is a single-direction layout concept whereby flex items are placed in horizontal rows or in vertical columns. The `flex-direction` property specifies the main axis, which in turn defines the horizontal or vertical direction in which flex items are placed in the flex container. The default value of `flex-direction` is `row`, which means that items are placed from left-to-right and from top-to-bottom (i.e., the order in which we read text on a page).

Here are the other values for `flex-direction`:

`row-reverse`: if the writing-mode specifies left-to-right, then the flex items will be laid out in a right-to-left fashion

`column`: if the writing system is horizontal, the flex items will be placed vertically

`column-reverse`: analogous to the column property, except the order is reversed

The CSS Flexbox model also enables you to expand the children of a flexbox to fill unused space, as well as shrink the children to avoid overflowing the parent. Moreover, you can create different layouts for different flexboxes in the same HTML Web page.

An Assortment of Flexbox Properties

Some useful flexbox properties that do not require prefixes include: `box-align`, `box-flex`, `box-ordinal-group`, `box-pack`, and `flex-flow`.

The `box-align` property (as well as other Flexbox properties) supports values such as `start`, `end`, `center`, `baseline`, and `stretch`, all of which enable you to specify the alignment of the elements in a flexbox. For example, `start` and `end` will left-justify and right-justify, respectively, a set of elements in a flexbox.

The `box-flex` property enables you to assign a greater relative weight to an element in a flexbox. The `box-ordinal-group` property enables you to change the default ordering of a set of elements in a flexbox. You can also use the `display` property and specify the value `box`.

You can use Flexbox properties to perform additional tasks:

• Use order to arrange flexbox children
• Use flex-basis to define dimensions on flexbox children
• Resize flexbox children correctly with flex-shrink and flex-grow
• Use flex-wrap and align-content to create grids

The next section contains an example of a Web page that contains some of the preceding Flexbox properties.

A WEB PAGE WITH FLEXBOX PROPERTIES

Listing 8.1 displays the contents of `SimpleFlexboxWK1.html` and Listing 8.2 displays the contents of `SimpleFlexboxWK1.css`, which illustrate how to use the flexbox properties in the list at the beginning of this section.

LISTING 8.1 SimpleFlexboxWK1.html

```
<!doctype html>
<html lang="en">
<head>
 <meta charset="utf-8">
 <title>Flexbox Layout</title>

 <link rel="stylesheet" href="simpleflex1wk.css">
</head>

<body>
  <div>
    <ul id="flex1">
      <li>Item11</li>
      <li>Item12</li>
      <li>Item13</li>
    </ul>

    <ul id="flex2">
      <li>Item21</li>
      <li>Item22</li>
      <li>Item23</li>
    </ul>

    <ul id="flex3">
      <li>Item31</li>
      <li>Item32</li>
      <li>Item33</li>
    </ul>
  </div>
 </div>
</body>
</html>
```

Listing 8.1 starts with a reference to a CSS stylesheet, followed by some boiler-plate HTML markup. The next section contains three unordered lists with an id attribute whose value is flex1, flex2, and flex3, respectively. Each unordered list is styled based on a matching selector in SimpleFlexboxWK1.css.

LISTING 8.2 SimpleFlexboxWK1.css

```
#flex1 {
 display: -webkit-box; width: 100%; height: 50px;
   background: #faa;
 -webkit-box-pack: center; -webkit-box-align: start;
}

#flex1 li {
  background: yellow; margin: 0 5px;
}

#flex1 li:nth-child(2) {
 -webkit-box-ordinal-group:1;
}

#flex2 {
```

```
display: -webkit-box; width: 100%; height: 50px;
   background: #aaf;
 -webkit-box-pack: center; -webkit-box-align: center;
}

#flex2 li {
 background: red; margin: 0 5px; -webkit-box-flex:1;
}

#flex2 li:nth-child(1) {
 -webkit-box-flex; -webkit-box-ordinal-group:1;
}

#flex3 {
 display: -webkit-box; width: 100%; height: 50px;
   background: #afa;
 -webkit-box-pack: center; -webkit-box-align: right;
}

#flex3 li {
background: #88f; margin: 0 5px; -webkit-box-flex:8;
}

#flex3 li:nth-child(1) {
 -webkit-box-flex:3; -webkit-box-ordinal-group:2;
}
```

Listing 8.2 contains nine selectors, with three selectors for each unordered list in Listing 8.1, and you can review the contents of the previous section for an explanation of the flexbox properties in the selectors in Listing 8.2.

RENDERING COLUMNS AND ROWS WITH FLEXBOX

Listing 8.3 displays the contents of Flexbox1.html, which illustrate how to render one set of HTML <div> elements as a column and another set of HTML <div> elements as a row by means of flex-related properties.

LISTING 8.3 Flexbox1.html

```
<!DOCTYPE html>
<html lang="en">
<head>
  <meta charset="utf-8" >
  <title>CSS3 Flexbox Examples</title>

  <style>
   #outer1 { display: block; }
   #outer2 { display: -webkit-box; }

   #outer1 > div {
     width: 200px;
     height : 50px;
     background-color: red;
     color: white;
     margin: 2px;
   }
```

```
      #outer2 > div {
        width: 200px;
        height : 50px;
        background-color: blue;
        color: white;
        margin: 2px;
      }
    </style>
</head>

<body>
  <div id="outer1">
    <div id="div1">div one</div>
    <div id="div2">div two</div>
    <div id="div3">div three</div>
  </div>

  <div id="outer2">
    <div id="div4">div four</div>
    <div id="div5">div five</div>
    <div id="div6">div six</div>
  </div>
 </body>
</html>
```

Listing 8.3 contains a <style> element with familiar standard CSS properties for styling the two <div> elements in the <body> element of Listing 8.3. In particular, the first selector renders the first <div> element as a column:

```
#outer1 { display: block; }
```

The only new functionality is the Flexbox-related CSS property in the second selector that renders the second <div> element as a row:

```
#outer2 { display: -webkit-box; }
```

Figure 8.1 displays the result of rendering Flexbox1.html in a Chrome browser on a MacBook.

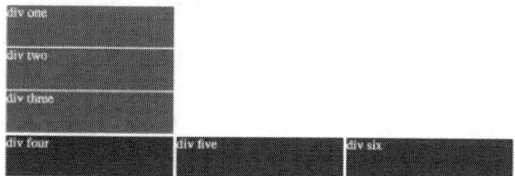

FIGURE 8.1 A CSS Flexbox example in Chrome on a MacBook.

As an example, consider the following <style> code block that specifies an HTML <div> element of width 300px that contains four <button> elements, each of which has width 80px:

```
<style>
 #div1 {
```

```
  display: flexbox;
  flex-flow: row wrap;
  width: 300px;
  }

 button {
  flex:80px 1;
  }
</style>

<div id="div1">
  <button id="button1">FreshTomatoes</button>
  <button id="button2">MincedGarlic</button>
  <button id="button3">FreshGinger</button>
  <button id="button4">OliveOil</button>
</div>
```

Since the HTML `<div>` element is not wide enough to accommodate the four buttons in a single row, the first three buttons are rendered in the first row and the fourth button is rendered as the lone element in the second row. In addition, the three buttons in the first row expand from `80px` to `100px`, and the fourth button expands from `80px` to `300px`.

This "expanding" behavior and the creation of a second row for the fourth button occur because the `flex-flow` property is set to "`row wrap`," which allows for a multi-line flexbox.

Useful Links for Flexbox

Additional information from the CSS Flexbox specification (work in progress) can be found at: *http://www.w3.org/TR/css3-flexbox/*.

A website that enables you to test flexbox code online is here: *http://flexbox.help/*.

A website with Flexbox "patterns" is here: *https://github.com/cjcenizal/flexbox-patterns*.

A CSS grid framework using Flexbox can be found at: *http://1000ch.github.io/grd/*.

A blog post with some useful Flexbox-related code snippets is here: *http://kyusuf.com/post/almost-complete-guide-to-flexbox-without-flexbox*.

CSS GRID LAYOUT

CSS Grid Layout enables you to control the layout of elements of an HTML web page in a grid-like fashion. The CSS Grid involves a display mode of `grid` and the use of a new unit of measure called `fr` ("fraction") for the unit length. You also specify the number of rows and columns using `pxs`, `ems`, or `auto` as the unit of measure.

For example, the following selector specifies four columns and three rows:

```
#mydiv {
  display: grid;
  grid-columns: 2fr 1fr 1fr 2fr;
```

```
   grid-rows: 50px auto 50px;
}
```

In the preceding selector, the first and last column occupy two-sixths of the width of the grid, whereas the middle pair of columns each occupy one-sixth of the grid width. The top and bottom rows both have a height of 50px, and the middle row occupies the remaining space.

Listing 8.4 displays the contents of CSSGrid1.html, which illustrates how to display a grid of button elements in an HTML Web page.

LISTING 8.4 CSSGrid1.html

```
<!DOCTYPE HTML>
<html>
 <head>
  <style>
    .grid {
      display: grid;
      grid-columns: repeat(4, 1fr);
      grid-rows: repeat(2, auto);
    }
  </style>
 </head>

 <body>
   <div class="grid">
     <header></header>
     <div class="content">
       <button id="btn1">Button1</button>
       <button id="btn2">Button2</button>
       <button id="btn3">Button3</button>
       <button id="btn4">Button4</button>
       <button id="btn5">Button5</button>
       <button id="btn6">Button6</button>
       <button id="btn7">Button7</button>
     </div>
   </div>
 </body>
</html>
```

Listing 8.4 contains a <style> element with a selector that styles the <div> element whose class attribute has the value grid. Currently there are seven <button> elements that are displayed in a single row. However, when you replace the two grid-related properties in Listing 8.4 with the following code lines, you will see a maximum of three buttons displayed in each row:

```
grid-template-columns: repeat(4, 1fr);
grid-template-rows: repeat(2, auto);
```

Figure 8.2 displays the result of rendering CSS3Grid1.html in a Chrome browser on a MacBook.

FIGURE 8.2 CSS3 Grid in a Chrome browser on a MacBook.

As you can probably see, CSS Grid Layout supports sophisticated layout definitions whose layout is far from obvious. For example, the following selector specifies four columns and three rows:

```
body {
    grid-columns: * * (0.5in * *)[2];
    grid-rows: 20% *;
    columns:3; column-gap:0.5in;
}
```

The preceding CSS selector contains the following information:

- An explicit grid is specified
- The parenthetical expression is a repeating pattern
- The integer in square brackets is the number of repetitions
- The asterisk syntax represents a proportional length, which means that each "*" is assigned equal space allocation

You can get additional information from the CSS Grid Layout specification (work in progress) at: *http://dev.w3.org/csswg/css3-grid-layout/* and *http://www.w3.org/TR/css3-grid/*.

IMPROVING HTML5 WEB PAGE PERFORMANCE

Performance is always an important consideration, and although a detailed and lengthy discussion is beyond the constraints of this book, it's important to be aware of some of the techniques that are available:

- Concatenate JavaScript/CSS files into a single file
- Use file compression (minification)
- Use of spritesheets
- Use base64 encoding of images
- Defer the loading of JavaScript files

A good blog post regarding the use of base64 for encoding images is here: *http://davidbcalhoun.com/2011/when-to-base64-encode-images-and-when-not-to?goback=%2Egde_2071438_member_234328886*.

You can defer the loading of JavaScript files by placing <script> tags at the end of the <body> element in a Web page.

Load CSS stylesheets asynchronously, as shown here: *http://filamentgroup.github.io/loadCSS/test/preload.html*.

You can also explore RequireJS, which is a JavaScript toolkit for asynchronously downloading JavaScript files (as well as managing JavaScript dependencies), and its home page is here: *http://requirejs.org/*.

CSS-RELATED PERFORMANCE

CSS3 provides wonderful functionality, such as rounded corners, as well as 2D and 3D graphics and animation effects. However, CSS3 features can differ in terms of performance, which obviously affects the performance of an HTML5 Web page.

Recall that you can guarantee that the GPU will be used on a device by using something such as `translate3D(0,0,0)`, which is essentially a "no operation." You can also replace 2D transforms by their corresponding 3D transforms. However, an indiscriminate use of 3D transforms can cause a page reflow or a page repaint, which has an adverse impact on performance.

Good articles regarding CSS paint times are here:

- *http://css-tricks.com/efficiently-rendering-css/*
- *http://www.html5rocks.com/en/tutorials/speed/css-paint-times/*
- *http://stickmanventures.com/labs/demo/spinning-gears-Chrome-preserve-3d/#*

Another interesting point pertains to the use of CSS3 translate versus absolute position in a CSS selector. Paul Irish compares these techniques here: *http://paulirish.com/2012/why-moving-elements-with-translate-is-better-than-pos-abs-topleft/*.

If you are interested in the lower level details about the painting process, CSS2 defines the order of the painting process, which is the order in which the elements are stacked in the "stacking contexts." This order affects painting because the stacks are painted from back to front. The stacking order of a block renderer is here:

- Background color
- Background image
- Border
- Children
- Outline

A more detailed explanation of the painting process can be found at the following: *http://www.html5rocks.com/en/tutorials/speed/unnecessary-paints/* and *http://www.html5rocks.com/en/tutorials/internals/howbrowserswork/*.

Steve Souders has written at least two performance-related books and has written many blog posts regarding performance, and it's definitely worth reading his work.

A CONDENSED COMPARISON OF CSS, SVG, AND CANVAS

CSS3 provides a) 2D/3D graphics/animation, b) GPU support, c) the ability to embed in an SVG <defs> element, d) "easing functions" for animation, and e) the capability to animate HTML elements.

SVG provides a) 2D graphics/animation, b) some GPU support, c) the ability to create arbitrary 2D shapes, d) custom <pattern>s, and e) grouping via the <g> element, and "easing functions in D3 (but SVG cannot animate HTML).

Canvas provides a) 2D graphics/animation, b) GPU support, c) the ability to update many small objects (games), and d) the option of working with video (use ThreeJS/WebGL for 3D animation).

CSS3+SVG is useful when a) you already have SVG-based data and b) you must support IE6 (this can be done with the Raphael toolkit but not D3).

CSS3+D3 is good for modern browsers and is also easier for defining event handlers and animation (probably also easier to maintain/enhance).

However, keep in mind that CSS3+SVG might not have GPU support (and perhaps consider D3 with BackboneJS/AngularJS/etc.).

Use CSS3 to create 3D animation effects with SVG as follows:

Step #1: create an SVG document
Step #2: create an SVG <defs> element
Step #3: create CSS3 selectors with CSS3 3D animation effects and put them in a <style> element
Step #4: insert the <style> element in the <defs> element
Step #5: set the "class" attribute in SVG elements so that it matches a CSS3 selector in the <style> element

Note that you can also reference an external CSS stylesheet in an SVG document.

Modern browsers support the <canvas> element. Use CSS3 with HTML5 Canvas by inserting a <canvas> element in a Web page and then use JavaScript APIs to create 2D shapes, all of which are rendered in a <canvas> element. Keep in mind that HTML5 <canvas> does not provide a DOM. However, CSS3 selectors can match the HTML5 <canvas> element. An article that explains how to trace Canvas calls is here: *http://www.html5rocks.com/en/tutorials/canvas/inspection/*.

Which Is Faster: CSS3/Canvas/SVG?

HTML5 Canvas is often faster than SVG for showing polygons and many small objects, but CSS3 is faster than Canvas for simple animation: *http://phrogz.net/tmp/image_move_speed.html*.

Moreover, CSS3 is faster than SVG for gradients, and D3 is better/faster than SVG for "follow the mouse." The preceding rules are general guidelines: make sure that you test/compare the performance characteristics of a Web page, especially if you develop for mobile devices.

HTML WEB PAGES AND BINARY IMAGES

Various factors can adversely affect the performance of an HTML Web page, which includes the download time for binary files. According to the following website, the average Web page is 1.8 megabytes, with 60% of the size resulting from images: *http://httparchive.org/interesting.php*.

Performance can be improved via several techniques, such as image format choice (discussed in another section), CSS spritesheets, preprocessing, deferred loading, caching, and CDNs. The following subsections discuss the first two techniques.

Selecting a File Format

As you know, SVG is a vector-based format, whereas other file formats involve binary data. Despite the advantages of SVG, there are several performance-related points to keep in mind. First, the process of rendering SVG in a browser is slower (partly because of the conversion process) than small binary files. Second, bitmaps on mobile devices involve the GPU, whereas SVG on mobile devices does not always involve the GPU. Third, use a tool for optimizing SVG files (as well as binary files).

With the preceding points in mind, SVG is well-suited for assets in a Web page that need to be scalable (SVG will always render them without "jaggies"). If scalability is not a requirement, then PNG files are an option. JPEG files are well-suited for photographs.

A good description of various file formats (and their trade-offs) is available here: *https://forums.adobe.com/thread/1640828*.

Optimizing SVG and Binary Files

The following website is useful for optimizing SVG files (and also provides downloadable command-line versions of the tool): *https://jakearchibald. github.io/svgomg/*.

You can also optimize binary assets using command-line tools such as this one: *https://imageoptim.com/command-line.html*.

The following link contains a tabular-based comparison of the compression rates of binary files by several tools: *http://jamiemason.github.io/ImageOptim-CLI/*.

CSS Spritesheets

CSS spritesheets involve the creation of one binary image that contains multiple binary images. Only a single HTTP request is required for downloading one spritesheet, which is more efficient than multiple HTTP requests for downloading the individual images separately.

A particular image in a spritesheet is rendered in a Web page by specifying the relative offset of the image in the spritesheet. Manually calculating the offsets is a tedious and error-prone process. Fortunately, there are online tools that create spritesheets and automatically calculate the necessary offsets for the individual images. One commercial tool (USD 20 for a single user) is Zwoptext, and its home page is here: *https://zwopple.com/zwoptex/*.

SpriteMe is a free tool for generating spritesheets and the accompanying CSS, and its home page is here: *www.spriteme.org*.

An article with best practices for spritesheets is here: *http://webdesign. tutsplus.com/articles/css-sprite-sheets-best-practices-tools-and-helpful-appli- cations--webdesign-8340.*

If you need to resize any of your images, ImageMagick is an excellent com- mand line tool for such a task, and its home page is here: *http://www.ima- gemagick.org/script/convert.php.*

After resizing the images, you can create a new spritesheet with the modi- fied images using a command line tool such as Glue: *http://glue.readthedocs. org/en/latest/.*

Perform an Internet search for other tools and then compare their features to determine which tools support your requirements.

The "Blur Up" Technique for Rendering Background Images

This technique involves an initial display of a small image, followed by scaling that image and simultaneously applying a Gaussian blur filter (filters are discussed in Chapter 2). The details of this technique are described here: *https://css-tricks.com/the-blur-up-technique-for-loading-background-images/.*

An example of this technique is here: *http://codepen.io/thatemil/pen/yY- maqG/.*

One interesting aspect of this technique pertains to the filter: you can use base64, CSS, or SVG for the filter definition. Another point of interest is the possibility of using this technique in progressive images (described in the next section).

Incidentally, the Facebook engineering team uses this technique to load cover photo previews in their native applications.

Progressive Images

Another technique for loading images in an HTML Web page involves progressive images. This technique involves downloading and displaying an initial version of an image that has a lower resolution, and then "progressively" downloading and redisplaying the image until the full resolution is rendered.

Interestingly, this technique was available in 2008 (and possibly earlier), and recently there has been a resurgence of interest in progressive images. However, the adoption rate of progressive images is still quite low. One possi- bility is mentioned in the following article that performed various tests involv- ing images with three different formats: *http://www.webperformancetoday. com/2014/09/17/progressive-image-rendering-good-evil/.*

Although there are no definitive conclusions in the preceding article, there is an interesting quote:

"When, as with the Progressive JPEG method, image rendition is a two-stage process in which an initially coarse image snaps into sharp focus, cognitive fluency is inhibited and the brain has to work slightly harder to make sense of what is being displayed."

Based on the preceding quote, perhaps the reaction of users to progressive images involves a combination of cognitive and subjective considerations.

If you are interested in learning about four ways in which binary files can be transmitted, the following link contains some interesting information: *http:// blog.codinghorror.com/progressive-image-rendering/*.

Another initiative to optimize Web pages is Google AMP (Accelerated Mobile Pages), which dramatically restricts the type of content that is allowed in an initial download of a Web page. Google AMP is discussed in the next chapter.

Web Fonts

Browsers download Web Fonts while rendering Web pages, and then those fonts are applied to the text in the Web page. A collection of Web Fonts is available here: *http://webfonts.info/*.

An example of including a Web Font in its style sheet is shown here:

```
<link rel='stylesheet' type='text/css'
href='http://fonts.googleapis.com/
css?family=Archivo+Narrow'>
```

Web Fonts can adversely affect performance of an HTML Web page when they are downloaded from a remote website. An online presentation regarding the performance of Web Fonts is here: *https://speakerdeck.com/bramstein/ web-fonts-performance*.

What to Do?

At this point it's probably clear that there is no one-size-fits-all formula for designing optimized HTML Web pages. However, one point is clear: after experimenting with various techniques, you need to test the performance of your Web pages in order to determine what will be optimal for your website.

OVERVIEW OF WEB ANIMATION APIS

Web animations can be performed in various ways, such as:

- `jQuery animate()`
- `requestAnimationFrame`
- `GreenSock and Velocity`
- `CSS Transitions and Keyframe Animations`
- `SVG Animation`
- `setTimeout/setInterval`

Web Animations are a set of standards to unify CSS and JavaScript animations. The key idea to remember is that Web Animations provide GPU-based animation through JavaScript.

The Web Animations API provides an animation player that supports the following methods and features:

```
play(), pause(), finish(), and cancel()
```

```
playState
reverse()
currentTime
playbackRate
```

The following code block illustrates how to create a player object with animation:

```
var player = document.getElementById('toAnimate').animate([
    { transform: 'scale(1)' },
    { transform: 'scale(.6)' }
  ], {
    duration: 700, //milliseconds
    iterations: Infinity, //or a number
    direction: 'normal', //'alternate', 'reverse', ...
    fill: 'forwards', //'backwards', 'both', 'none', 'auto'
    delay: 10, //milliseconds
    easing: 'ease-in-out', //'linear', 'ease-in', ...
  });
```

The following code block illustrates how to create a player object that animates multiple frames:

```
var player = document.getElementById('toAnimate2').
animate([
    {transform: 'scale(1)',   opacity: 1,   offset: 0 },
    {transform: 'scale(.5)',  opacity: .5, offset: .3333},
    {transform: 'scale(.66)', opacity: .66,offset: .6666},
    {transform: 'scale(.6)',  opacity: .6, offset: 1 }
  ], {
    duration: 700,
    easing: 'linear',
    delay: 0,
    iterations: 3,
    direction: 'alternate',
    fill: 'forwards'
  });
```

The next section contains a complete code sample that uses the Web Animation APIs.

AN EXAMPLE OF THE WEB ANIMATION APIS

This section contains a code sample that uses the Web Animations APIs in order to create animation effects with SVG elements. This sample is part of the following Github repository: *https://github.com/ocampesato/web-animations*.

You need to install bower and then invoke the command bower install in order to set up an environment on your machine, and the README.md file in the preceding repository contains detailed instructions.

Listing 8.5 displays the contents of AnimArchOvals1.html, which illustrates how to use the Web Animation APIs in order to create animation effects with a set of ellipses that follow the path of an Archimedean spiral.

LISTING 8.5 AnimArchOvals1.html

```
<!doctype html>
<html>
 <head>
  <meta name="viewport"
    content="width=device-width, minimum-scale=1.0,
initial-scale=1.0, user-scalable=yes">
  <title>Archimedean Graphics</title>

  <script src="web-animations-next.min.js"></script>
  <script src="bower_components/platform/platform.js">
  </script>

  <link rel="import" href="bower_components/polymer/
                            polymer.html">
  <link rel="import" href="PolyArchOvals1.html">
 </head>

 <body unresolved>
   <svg-graphics id="main" width="800" height="600">
   </svg-graphics>

   <script>
       var elem = document.querySelector('#main');
       var player = elem.animate([
           {opacity: 0.5, transform: "rotate(-225deg)"},
           {opacity: 0.5, transform: "scale(0.5)"},
           {opacity: 1.0, transform:
                               "translate(300px,200px)"},
           {opacity: 1.0, transform: "scale(1.5)"}
       ], {
           direction: 'alternate',
           duration: 2000,
           iterations: Infinity
       });
   </script>
 </body>
</html>
```

Listing 8.5 initializes the variable `player` that specifies four animation effects involving a combination of the opacity attribute and four transform functions. The animation effects last for two seconds and repeat indefinitely in an alternating back-and-forth fashion.

OTHER TOOLKITS FOR JS WEB ANIMATIONS

This section contains brief descriptions of JavaScript toolkits that support animation effects.

The GSAP Toolkit provides sophisticated animation and tweening effects. GSAP is pure JavaScript (no "special" or proprietary language) for creating animation effects, and its home page is here: *http://greensock.com/gsap*.

Note that GSAP does not convert fonts or create SVG artwork. GSAP TweenLite is the core toolkit that can animate CSS properties (among other things), and TweenMax is a superset of TweenLite with advanced features. TimelineLite is a sequencing tool, and TimelineMax is a superset of TimelineLite. GSAP also supports easing functions and various plugins are available. More samples are here: *http://greensock.com/examples-showcases.*

Some eye-candy code samples that combine SVG, GSAP, and ReactJS are here: *https://github.com/ocampesato/react-svg-gsapi.*

PostCSS is a very small toolkit that contains only a CSS parser, a CSS node tree API, a source map generator, and a node tree stringifier. All of the style transformations are performed by plugins, which are plain JS functions. Each plugin receives a CSS node tree, transforms it, and then returns the modified tree.

PostCSS works with the same principles of preprocessors such as Sass and LESS: *http://www.smashingmagazine.com/2015/12/introduction-to-postcss/.*

You can use the [cssnext] plugin pack and write future CSS code right now:

```
:root {
    --mainColor: #ffbbaaff;
}
@custom-media     --mobile (width <= 640px);
@custom-selector :--heading h1, h2, h3, h4, h5, h6;

.post-article :--heading {
    color: color( var(--mainColor) blackness(+20%) );
}
@media (--mobile) {
    .post-article :--heading {
        margin-top: 0;
    }
}
```

Sequence.js is a JavaScript toolkit that supports a built-in CSS framework for creating animation effects, and its home page is here: *http://www.sequencejs. com/.*

Content transitions are defined in terms of CSS, and also involve the GPU for hardware acceleration to create very smooth animation effects.

A detailed tutorial about sequence.js is here: *https://davidwalsh.name/creating-animated-product-slider-sequencejs.*

A codepen demo of sequence.js is here: *http://codepen.io/IanLunn/pen/ qObKVR.*

Finally, the JavaScript-based open source toolkit mojs.io enables you to create very nice animation effects, and its home page is here: *http://mojs.io/.*

WORKING WITH CHROME INSPECTOR

Chrome Inspector is a powerful tool that enables you to perform various tasks. In particular, Chrome Inspector makes it easy for you to do the following:

1. View the computed CSS properties of any element in the DOM
2. Modify CSS properties and see the changes take effect

3. Save the CSS stylesheet with the CSS modifications

4. Load/view a CSS stylesheet in the Sources tab

5. Find performance bottlenecks

This section provides details for some of the items in the preceding list. Now launch `Threed2Hover1.html` in a Chrome browser, and then navigate to `View->Developer->JavaScript Console` in order to view the contents of Chrome Inspector. The `Elements` tab and the `Sources` tab are discussed in this section, and you can investigate the other tabs after you complete this section.

Figure 8.3 displays the contents of `ChromeInspector.png`, which is a screenshot of Chrome Inspector after launching the HTML Web page `Three-d2Hover1.html`.

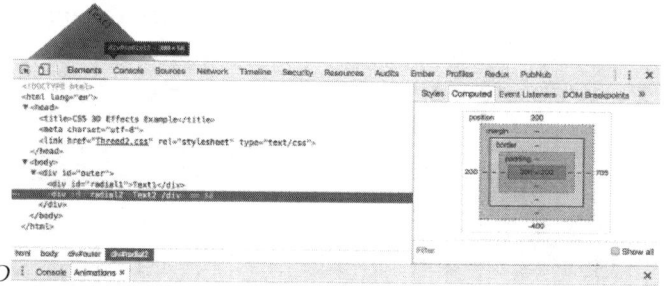

FIGURE 8.3 An example of the contents of Chrome Inspector.

Click on the `Elements` tab and you will see the contents of the DOM for the current HTML Web page that is in the browser. As you expand the various elements, notice how the top portion of your browser session highlights some properties of the currently selected item in the DOM.

Click on the `Sources` tab and click on the file `Threed2Hover1.css` in order to see the contents of this file. On the right side of the screen you will see various tabs displayed. Click on the `Computed` tab and you will see the values of properties that have been set for any element in the DOM. For each HTML element, the values of the computed properties are the "aggregate" result of the CSS selectors that match that HTML element.

Chrome Inspector enables you to add new CSS selectors that are applied dynamically to the current HTML Web page. Click on the `Styles` tab (on the left of the `Computed` tab) and then click on the plus ("+") button that is located at the right-most edge of your browser, in a row of buttons that is below the row that contains the `Styles` tab. As a simple example, add this CSS selector:

```
body {
   background-color: blue;
}
```

Notice that as you type the letters of the color `blue`, Chrome updates the background color with a color that matches the current input string.

Now click on the `Timeline` tab and you will see a "`Capture:`" option that enables you to collect memory information about timelines, and also capture screenshots while doing so. Click on the dark circle that is to the left of (and below) the `Elements` tab whenever you want to `Record` information, and click on the circle to its right when you want to clear recording information. Experiment with these options and perform some recordings so that you can familiarize yourself with the details of capturing performance-related details.

SUMMARY

In this chapter, you learned about Project Houdini, which is a workgroup whose goal is to achieve consistency and extensibility in CSS in modern browsers. Then you learned about FlexBox and Grid Layout, and some performance techniques for binary images. Next you saw a comparison of CSS3, SVG, and HTML5 `Canvas`, along with an example of how to use the Web Animation APIs. In addition, you learned about performance techniques, spritesheets, and several techniques for rendering binary images in Web pages.

CHAPTER 9

DESIGNING MOBILE APPS

The purpose of this chapter is to provide some guidelines for designing good HTML5 mobile applications. This chapter discusses aspects of the UI experience, and how to create aesthetically appealing mobile Web applications. In addition, this chapter covers some of the toolkits that can help you support the desired functionality without sacrificing important design considerations. Some of the sections in this chapter involve CSS3 Media Queries from Chapter 5, so you might need to review the relevant sections in that chapter prior to reading some of the sections in this chapter.

The first part of this chapter discusses some of the major aspects of the mobile metaphor, which is touch-oriented instead of mouse-oriented. The second part of this chapter delves into design-related aspects of mobile forms. The final portion of this chapter discusses Google AMP (Accelerated Mobile Pages) and Progressive Mobile Apps (also developed by Google). Although Google AMP is still a new technology, it's relevant because Google AMP supports some CSS as well as most SVG elements.

Keep in mind the following points when you read this chapter. First, this chapter contains almost no code samples because its focus is stylistic considerations. Second, this chapter does not delve into toolkits for creating hybrid mobile applications (a detailed discussion is beyond the scope of this book). However, PhoneGap (Cordova) is a very popular toolkit, and it has influenced other mobile toolkits. Ionic (acquired by IBM) is a toolkit that uses Angular 2 for creating hybrid mobile applications and also uses PhoneGap internally. Lots of online resources are available for PhoneGap, Ionic, and other toolkits for hybrid mobile applications.

Incidentally, PhoneGap and Ionic applications do rely on a DOM structure, but there are toolkits and products for developing mobile applications that do not use a DOM. In particular, React Native from Facebook and Xamarin (acquired by Microsoft) are two such products. Visit the respective Web sites of these toolkits for code samples and tutorials.

WHAT IS GOOD MOBILE DESIGN?

The answer to this simple question is more complex than you might think, but there are some guidelines to help you make design decisions for hybrid HTML5 mobile applications (and also native applications, such as iOS and Android, which are outside the scope of this book). As you will see, some of these guidelines include touch-orientation, performance and responsiveness, detecting screen sizes, resizing assets, and determining the actual content.

The next several sections provide more information about these and other important factors, and then discuss toolkits or provide code snippets that can help you implement the desired functionality.

IMPORTANT FACETS OF MOBILE WEB DESIGN

Some of the important considerations for designing hybrid HTML5 mobile applications are here:

- A touch-oriented design (not mouse-oriented)
- Improving response times of user gestures
- Detecting different screen sizes (especially for Android devices)
- Resizing assets (such as images)
- Determining the content of a Web page

Instead of handling mouse clicks, mobile web applications handle touch-related events (single tap and multiple taps) and user gestures (swipe, flick, pan, and so forth).

Fortunately, jQuery Mobile provides a virtualization of events that takes care of mouse events and touch events through a single set of APIs. This virtualization simplifies your code: you only need to handle one set of events.

A TOUCH-ORIENTED DESIGN

You might think that you can accomplish this goal simply by replacing all mouse-related events with their touch-related counterparts. Although this is a good starting point, there are several caveats to this approach. First, there is no touch event that is the counterpart for a mouse-based hover event. Consequently, CSS stylesheets with selectors of the type `#myDiv:hover` will work correctly on laptops and desktops, but they do not work correctly on mobile devices.

Second, when users touch a mobile screen with one of their fingers, the second gesture could be one of the following:

1. Touch up
2. Touch hold

3. Touch move

4. Swipe gesture

For this reason, there is a delay (roughly 300 milliseconds) to allow for a second event. The first event (touch down) can be combined with the second event to determine the correct user gesture. However, this delay can affect the perceived responsiveness of a mobile web application. Fortunately, there are JavaScript toolkits that improve touch-related responsiveness of mobile web applications, which is the topic of the next section.

IMPROVING RESPONSE TIMES OF USER GESTURES

There are several toolkits for eliminating the 300-millisecond delay between the first touch event and the second touch event. The first JavaScript toolkit with nice touch-related functionality is `fastclick.js`, and its home page is here: *https://github.com/ftlabs/fastclick.*

Mobile browsers wait about 300 milliseconds after an initial tap event in order to determine if users will perform a double tap. Since FastClick eliminates the 300-millisecond delay between a physical tap and the firing of a click event on mobile browsers, mobile applications feel more responsive.

Listing 9.1 displays the contents of the HTML5 Web page `FastClick1.html`, which illustrates how to use `fastclick.js` in a Web page.

LISTING 9.1 FastClick1.html

```
<html>
<head>
  <meta charset="utf-8">
  <script src='/path/to/fastclick.js'></script>
</head>

<body>
  <script>
    window.addEventListener('load', function() {
        FastClick.attach(document.body);
    }, false);
  </script>
</body>
</html>
```

Listing 9.1 is straightforward: include a `<script>` element that references fastclick.js and then add an event listener that invokes the `attach()` method of `fastclick.js` during a browser load event.

You can also use `fastclick.js` with mobile Web applications that use jQuery Mobile, and a detailed description is provided here: *http://forum. jquery.com/topic/how-to-remove-the-300ms-delay-when-clicking-on-a-link-in-jquery-mobile.*

RESIZING ASSETS IN MOBILE WEB APPLICATIONS

There are at least two common techniques for detecting screen sizes, which in turn is related to resizing assets. The first technique involves CSS3 Media Queries to load different CSS stylesheets for different screen widths. The second technique is to use JavaScript to set different CSS properties for different screen sizes.

When you place assets (such as PNG files) on an HTML5 Web page in a mobile Web application, you need to decide how to handle the following situations for your mobile web application:

1. Switching from portrait to landscape (or vice versa)
2. Deploying to mobile devices with different screen sizes
3. Resizing text strings and text areas
4. Scaling non-binary images (such as SVG)

You need to address the preceding situations whenever you create an HTML5 Web page that includes not only PNG files, but also other types of assets, such as embedded SVG documents or HTML5 <canvas> elements.

In the case of rendering text strings, how do you determine the correct font size? Even if you use em for the unit of measure, you don't know the DPI resolution of a particular device. Of course, you could make an educated guess and decide that text will be rendered with 14em for a mobile phone and 16em for a tablet (or phablet), but the increasing variety of screens with different DPIs means that you can't guarantee that your choice will be correct in all cases.

In the case of SVG documents that are embedded in an HTML5 Web page, you can use a CSS-based technique for automatically resizing the contents of SVG documents in an HTML5 Web page with this code snippet:

```
<div style="background-size: contain">
```

A detailed description of this technique is here: *https://developer.mozilla.org/ en-US/docs/Web/CSS/background-size.*

DETERMINING THE CONTENT LAYOUT FOR MOBILE WEB PAGES

Some design considerations for determining the content of a Web page are here:

• Provide a single column of text for smart phones
• Remove extra links and content
• Remove items and sidebars/footers
• Avoid absolute sizes
• Set wrapper widths to percentages
• Set paragraphs to display block

Keep in mind that the preceding points are guidelines and not absolute rules. For example, some smart phones in landscape mode can accommodate two columns, depending on the width of the columns, and many tablets can display two columns in portrait mode. Some people recommend that you reduce the amount of scrolling that is required in a screen, but many users are accustomed to frequent scrolling on a mobile device (especially on smart phones). When in doubt, create two (or possible more) layouts and get feedback from users to determine which layout might have greater appeal to a broad audience. If you still cannot decide which layout design is best for your purposes, perhaps you can benefit from "A/B testing," which is described here: *http://en.wikipedia.org/wiki/A/B_testing*.

MOBILE DESIGN FOR HTML WEB PAGES

There are several approaches to designing HTML Web pages for mobile devices, including "mobile first," "mobile only," and using a separate domain for mobile applications.

A "mobile first" approach ensures that an HTML Web page will render correctly on a mobile device. However, you need to take into account different screen sizes among mobile devices, such as smart phones, "phablets," and tablets. This detail is particularly evident with Android mobile devices (and to a lesser extent it's true for iOS devices).

A "mobile only" approach still requires you to take into account different screen sizes on mobile devices, but in this scenario you do not need to contend with HTML Web pages for laptops or desktops. Keep in mind that this approach is far from trivial: it can involve a combination of client (or server) templates, local data stores, and efficient view-model binding that are provided by toolkits such as `BackboneJS`. Another point to consider is whether or not you can leverage NoSQL datastores, such as MongoDB.

A third approach is to use separate domains for mobile versus desktop Web pages. If you are developing thin mobile web applications (i.e., Web pages that are hosted on a server and accessed by various device types), this approach provides several advantages. First, this makes your mobile site easier to find. Second, you can advertise the mobile URL separately from the URL for desktop devices. Third, users can switch between the "regular" website and the mobile website simply by changing the domain. Fourth, the code logic for detecting mobile users (and then sending them to a separate domain) is simpler than making modifications to CSS stylesheets.

Now that you have an overview of design considerations for mobile Web pages, let's take a look at an example of styling mobile forms, which is the topic of the next section.

HIGH-LEVEL VIEW OF STYLING MOBILE FORMS

When you render a mobile form, there are high-level techniques (such as how to display input fields) as well as techniques that are specific in nature (such as indicating required fields).

The following list contains some high-level techniques for rendering mobile forms:

- Using semantic markup
- Using a single column to display input fields (for smart phones)
- Deciding on label alignment (left or top)
- Grouping/chunking input fields
- Tooltips or information bubbles
- Displaying error messages
- Appropriate field width
- Suitable color scheme
- Tabs instead of radio buttons
- Handling long drop-down lists (use predictive search or links)
- Primary and secondary buttons
- Spacing between input elements
- Pop-up menu controls
- Voice input

Notice that there is no "reduce scrolling" in the previous list: users are accustomed to scrolling on smart phones and tablets. In addition, a single-column display was more important for smaller smart phones, but some smart phones can display two columns in landscape mode, and tablets are even more accommodating in terms of multiple columns of text.

If you render text in a left-to-right direction, then left-aligned labels enable you to place more input fields in a screen, and they are also easier to scan during field input, but they don't work well with long input fields. Top-aligned labels have the opposite advantages and disadvantages of left-aligned labels. Yet another technique is to use inline labeling, which essentially means that the "text prompt" for the input field provides a suggestion for the type of data that is expected.

SPECIFIC TECHNIQUES FOR STYLING MOBILE FORMS

In addition to the design techniques that are listed in the previous section, you can use some or all of these specific techniques:

- Use CSS to style input fields differently
- Provide labels for input fields
- Specify keyboard types for input fields
- Provide default or suggested values for input fields
- Use constraints for numeric fields
- Indicate required fields
- Validate each field after user input
- Utilize password masking
- Employ field zoom

The following subsections provide additional details for some of the bullet items in the preceding list.

Use CSS to Style Input Fields Differently

There are two steps involved. The first step is to apply the default styling and then apply your own styling rules. The second step is to use the `[type=]` attribute selector to apply different styles to different input fields.

As a specific example you can use the `-webkit-appearance` property to remove the default styling for all input elements, as shown here:

```
input, textarea, select {
    -webkit-appearance: none;
}
```

Next, specify your own CSS styles that depend on the type of input field, as outlined here:

```
input[type=checkbox]
    /* specify styles for checkbox */
}

input[type=radio] {
    /* specify styles for radio */
}

input[type=textarea] {
    /* specify styles for textarea */
}
```

You can use the preceding example as a guideline for defining CSS selectors to change the appearance of other HTML elements in your Web pages.

Specify Keyboard Types for Input Fields

HTML5 introduced the following new properties for the type attribute for input elements:

```
an email address: type='email'
a website address: type='url'
telephone number: type='tel'
```

The preceding types only work on mobile browsers (nothing will happen in a laptop or desktop browser).

The following example shows you how to specify different keyboards for input fields:

```
<form id="form1" name="form1" method="post" action="">
<label for="name">Name:</label><input name="name" id="name"
    type="text" /><br />
<label for="email">Email:</label><input name="email"
    id="email" type="email" /><br />
<label for="phone">Phone:</label><input name="phone"
    id="phone" type="tel" /><br />
```

```
<input name="submit" type="button" value="Submit" />
</form>
```

Different Countries and Languages

There are several points to keep in mind when you create applications for different countries and languages:

- Different phone formats in different countries
- Left-to-right versus right-to-left text input
- Culturally appropriate content

If you intend to publish Android applications that support multiple languages, the following link provides useful information: *http://developer.vodafone.com/ how-support-multiple-languages-android/*.

If you intend to publish iOS applications that support multiple countries and languages, Apple provides extensive information here: *https://developer. apple.com/internationalization/*.

The details of creating internationalized iOS mobile applications (such as how to create additional string resources) are here: *http://www.slideshare.net/ cxpartners/web-and-mobile-forms-design-userfriendly-2010-workshop*.

DESIGN-RELATED TOOLS AND ONLINE PATTERNS

`Balsamiq` is an online design tool, and its home page is here: *http://www. balsamiq.com/*.

`Balsamic Mockups` is a tool for rapidly creating wireframes, designed to reproduce the experience of sketching interfaces on a whiteboard. Since these mockups are on your computer, you can share them quickly and easily with other people.

Another toolkit for creating wireframes is `justinmind`, and its home page is here: *http://justinmind.com*.

Both of the preceding tools are free to use, and they have videos that illustrate how to use them.

Two websites that provide a collection of design patterns (the second is purely for mobile) are here: *http://pttrns.com* and *http://mobile-patterns.com*.

WORKING WITH FONT SIZES AND UNITS OF MEASURE

If you have already worked with CSS stylesheets, then you are already familiar with different units that are available for expressing font sizes for text in HTML5 Web pages. Several units are available, including em, rem, px, pt, and %.

The relationship among these units is as follows:

```
1em = 12pt = 16px = 100%
```

Pixel units (px) are very common in Web pages (especially for desktops and laptops), and they can vary in terms of their resolution and their DPI (dots per inch). Pixel units are virtual screen pixels rather than physical pixels. One point to keep in mind is that the pixel unit does not scale correctly for visually-impaired readers.

You can use the px unit for text, images, borders, rounded corners, and drop shadows. However, if you are building a fluid layout that uses relative sizes, it's probably better to use the em unit or the % unit for text.

The em unit is becoming more popular, especially on mobile devices, because this unit is well suited for scaling a Web page. Unlike the px unit, the em unit is relative to its parent element in a Web page. It might be helpful to think of the px unit as "global" whereas the em unit is "local."

One useful technique is to specify the value 62.5% for the <body> element. Since 62.5% equals the fraction 5/8, the product of 16px and 5/8 is 10px. The value 10px is a convenient "base point" for performing conversions quickly and easily between px units and em units in CSS selectors. For example, 1.5em is 15px, 2em is 20px, 2.5em is 25px, and so forth. In case you need help in performing conversions, an online em calculator is here: *http://riddle.pl/emcalc/* and *http://www.ready.mobi/launch.jsp?locale=en_EN.*

Additional useful information is here: *http://www.w3.org/QA/Tips/font-size.*

WHAT IS GOOGLE AMP?

Google AMP is an open source initiative for rendering Web pages more quickly on mobile devices, and its home page is here: *https://www.ampproject.org/.*

The initial AMP specification was announced in October 2015, and code samples are available here: *https://github.com/ampproject/amphtml.*

Accelerated Mobile Pages can be loaded in any modern browser or Web view. However, AMPs impose a restricted subset of functionality compared to "regular" HTML Web pages in order to reduce the time to load AMPS in a browser. Moreover, AMPs can be cached in the cloud, which can yield additional speed improvements.

Some of the AMP restrictions for AMP-compliant Web pages are here:

No developer-written or third-party JavaScript
No input elements of any kind, including standard input and text area
No external style sheets and only one style tag in the document head
No inline styles
Style rules must be at or below 50kb

Consumers of the AMP specification include content producers, who can create AMP Web pages that can be crawled, indexed, and displayed. The good news is that Google AMP supports most SVG elements, and perhaps additional support will be available in the future.

NOTE *Google AMP supports most SVG elements.*

You can think of AMP as a framework for creating mobile Web pages that consists of AMP HTML (a subset of HTML with AMP-specific elements), AMP JS (a JavaScript framework for AMP that disallows third-party JavaScript), and an optional AMP CDN (Content Delivery Network).

One of the goals of AMP is to support all published content in Accelerated Mobile Pages.

More information about AMP is available in the following FAQ: *https://www.ampproject.org/docs/support/faqs.html.*

The RAIL Framework

RAIL is an acronym for the following time-based measurements: Reaction time (100ms), Animation time (60FPS), Idle time (<50ms), and Load time (< one second). The parenthesized numbers in the preceding sentence are the goals of the respective time measurements. The availability of functionality such as Service Workers (albeit an experimental technology) in modern browsers will assist in reaching the RAIL goal of adequate performance of Web pages.

Currently there is partial support for Service Workers in Chrome, Opera, and Firefox, and more information about Service Workers is here: *https://developer.mozilla.org/en-US/docs/Web/API/Service_Worker_API.*

Styles in AMP

All styles must appear in a `style` tag in the head of the document, and the style tag must contain the `amp-custom` attribute.

```
<amp-lightbox id="lightbox" class="lightbox"
layout="nodisplay">
    <div class="lightbox-content">
      <amp-img
        src="https://cdn.auth0.com/website/jobs/myimage.jpg"
        width="2000"
        height="1035"
        layout="responsive">
      </amp-img>
      <p> some text in a paragraph </p>
    </div>
</amp-lightbox>
```

AMP components support for ads includes: A9, AdReactor, AdSense, AdTech, and Doubleclick. Companies involved in Google AMP include Twitter, Pinterest, WordPress.com, Chartbeat, Parse.ly, Adobe Analytics, and LinkedIn.

The Status of HTML Elements and Core AMP Components

Elements prohibited by AMP include:

base, frame, frameset
object, param, applet
embed, form, script (*)

input, textarea, select, option

(*) unless it's of type "application/ld+json"

Allowed HTML elements (with caveats in some cases) include: button, link, style, most SVG elements, and some support for stylesheets.
Built-in "core" AMP components are:

amp-img, amp-audio, amp-video
amp-pixel, amp-anim, amp-iframe
amp-carousel, amp-lightbox, amp-ad
amp-instagram, amp-twitter, amp-youtube

> **NOTE** *Built-in components are always available in an AMP document and they have an* <amp-*> *element.*

The Core/Extended AMP components include the following:

amp-img amp-audio amp-video
amp-pixel amp-anim amp-iframe
amp-carousel amp-lightbox amp-ad
amp-instagram amp-twitter amp-youtube

Elements replaced by AMP include img (amp-img), video (amp-video), audio (amp-audio), and iframe (amp-iframe).
An example of the <amp-img> element is here:

```
<amp-img
  src="https://mysite/myimage.jpg"
  width="2000"
  height="1035"
  layout="responsive">
</amp-img>
```

An AMP extended component involves loading the JavaScript in the <head> element. Navigate to the following link to see an example of a simple AMP Web page: *https://www.ampproject.org/docs/get_started/create/basic_markup.html.*

WHAT ARE PROGRESSIVE WEB APPS?

Progressive Web Apps are based on pages in browser tabs, and they use the app shell model to give them a "look and feel" that is similar to native mobile applications. Progressive Web Apps are responsive (they work with any form factor), safe (served via HTTPS), and always up-to-date because of their use of Service Workers.

A progressive web app performs the following steps:

1. Registers a service worker

2. Runs on HTTPS (required in order to prevent man-in-the-middle attacks)

3. Creates a JSON-based app manifest file with information about the app

Service Workers consist of a collection of APIs (by Google) for offline access and Web push notifications. The manifest file contains metadata, such as icons, orientation, and so forth. Note that the Polymer startup kit contains a valid manifest file. Chrome for Android and Opera for Android allow you to save the app on your homescreen, which means it looks just like a native application on your homescreen. You can open the app with a default orientation. A key point is that the app works like a "normal" website in browsers that do not support progressive apps. An example of a progressive web app manifest is here: *https://mobiforge.com/design-development/web-app-manifests-usher-new-wave-progressive-apps-to-your-homescreen*.

IMPROVING HTML5 WEB PAGE PERFORMANCE

Performance is always a very important consideration, and although a detailed and lengthy discussion is beyond the constraints of this book, it's important to be aware of some of the techniques that are available:

- Concatenate JavaScript/CSS files into a single file
- Use file compression (minification)
- Use of spritesheets
- Use base64 encoding of images
- Defer the loading of JavaScript files

A good blog post regarding the use of base64 for encoding images is here: *http://davidbcalhoun.com/2011/when-to-base64-encode-images-and-when-not-to?goback=%2Egde_2071438_member_234328886*.

You can defer the loading of JavaScript files by placing `<script>` tags at the end of the `<body>` element in a Web page.

You can also explore `RequireJS`, which is a JavaScript toolkit for asynchronously downloading JavaScript files (as well as managing JavaScript dependencies), and its home page is here: *http://requirejs.org/*.

Steve Souders has written at least two performance-related books and has written many blog posts regarding performance, and it's definitely worth reading his work.

USEFUL LINKS

The following links are helpful for testing Mobile applications:

- *http://css3test.com/*
- *http://www.css3.info/selectors-test/*

- *http://quirksmode.org/html5/tests/video.html*
- *http://double.co.nz/video_test/*
- *http://www.terrillthompson.com/tests/html5-audio.html*

Other resources include *www.stackoverflow.com* and videos by Paul Irish.

A more recent website is HTML5 Please, which consists of contributions from well-known industry people: *http://html5please.com.*

The preceding website provides an input field where you can specify HTML5 and CSS3 features to determine if they are ready for use, and also see how to use them.

The W3C provides a free online validation service for HTML Web pages, including HTML5 Web pages: http://*validator.w3.org/#validate_by_uri+with_ options.*

The preceding website enables you to validate an URL, a file, or direct input of code.

The following website provides "boilerplate" templates for HTML5 email input fields (and also templates for CSS and jQuery): *http://favbulous.com/ post/848/6-useful-web-development-boilerplates.*

SUMMARY

In this chapter, you learned about the touch-oriented metaphor of the mobile environment, along with design-related aspects of mobile forms. In addition, you saw how to improve the response time of user gestures via fast-click.js, and also the fact that you can use CSS3 Media Queries and JavaScript to detect the screen sizes of mobile devices. You also learned about Google AMP and its support for many SVG elements. Next you learned about Progressive Mobile Apps, and a high-level view of performance-related details.

INDEX